PRET

Nonsense, Shenanigans and
Tactful Life Domination

ALI FARRELL

SEA STREET PUBLISHING

SC ISBN: 9781733078405
Hardcover ISBN: 978-1-7330784-1-2
Ebook ISBN: 978-1-7330784-2-9
Audiobook ISBN: 978-1-7330784-3-6

Printed in the United States of America

Sea Street Publishing
32 Sea Street
Camden, Maine 04843

www.PrettyCombatBook.Com

Cover Design: Vanessa Mendozzi

Editor: Tiffany White

Cover Photography: MacKenzie & Cal Farrell

CONTENTS

Introduction

Hey, thanks for reading my book! If you're here, you're probably a fellow badass looking to kick ass and take names in this crazy, exhausting, awesome thing we call life. I'm not a big fan of longwinded, twisting and turning stories to get to the final point in a nonfiction book, so I did my best to make this jam packed with value, rather than adding all the excruciating small details of my life that you don't give a flying hoot about—like my favorite ice cream flavor (I'd actually prefer buffalo wings), my mom's maiden name (okay, it's Troup, that's kind of important), or what I like in my coffee (I mean, just in case we ever hang out, it's your basic milk and sugar). Your time is precious, so let's get down to dominating.

The first section of this book talks about getting your mind right. I try not to get all hippie, spiritual, cosmic because I do in fact ♡ science and hard facts, but there's a source of energy that we simply must chat about.

The second section is about leveling up your life and kicking ass in every way. Simply put, it's a Mack Truck steaming toward you at full speed, about to rock your world with success, motivation, and fun facts for mastering life.

The third section is where we get into some juicy relationship gossip. The good, the bad, the ones who F-ed up. Their damage, my damage, and most importantly what I've learned along the way, cruising through this journey of love on my little struggle bus, which eventually led me to some serious happiness and decoding the relationship matrix for myself.

Sections four and five are written by my brilliant guest writers. They leave you with your mind wide open, urging you to step outside the box of "normal" to get exactly what you deserve.

In the sixth section, it's your turn. Time to take action. *You'll see.*

Many of the life lessons in this book have been learned the hard way, so buckle down for some nonsense, shenanigans, and tactful life domination.

To get us rolling, I want to mention some important words said by a smart person who left this world far too soon. My buddy Jillian Stupak had a best friend, Pat Padgett, who recently passed away from cancer at a young age. He left us with words that are so simple but so impactful on how we should strive to live our life each day. It seems consistent that when people are near the end, they finally have the clarity of exactly how they wished they had lived their life. Pat Padgett has been there and given us the gift of clarity before we reach that point. He gives us the chance to choose action while we still have the precious opportunity to live this life as we're meant to. If we have the invaluable knowledge of what will be most important to us in the end, let's take advantage and make a plan to act on it.

> *"So do me the honor of living your life like you really mean it. Go out and conquer your goals, do things that you're a little scared of, make awesome memories that give you cool stories to tell, and love. Love as much as possible, freely and genuinely. Love people, love activities, love scenes and ideas, and material things, and songs, and just love as much as you can. Enjoy your life. You only get one, and value your time, you never know how much of it you really have."*

> *—Pat Padgett*

So right now, let's actively make the decision to love hard, conquer our fears, and make some stories worth telling.

PART 1

MIND YOUR MINDSET:

LIVING A LIFE OF

VALUE AND INTENT

"The purpose of life, after all, is to live it, to taste experience to the utmost, to reach out eagerly and without fear for newer and richer experiences."

—*Eleanor Roosevelt*

It takes action to live a life of intent and value. Your everyday choices will either lead you to a life of fulfillment and freedom or a life of stress and struggle.

Many of us wake up, and the day immediately begins with an endless amount of work that has us knee deep in busyness throughout the day. That means instead of connecting with others, valuing the things around us, expressing gratitude, or taking the time to notice and love life, we're wading through . . . well, crap. Listen, you and I could do laundry, dishes, and house cleaning until the cows come home. In fact, it's a never-ending battle royale of laundry warfare. FYI, the laundry always wins, which means today I'm hiding in the trenches and sneaking some whiskey while the children's dirty clothes bombs rain down around me. Don't judge. However, do you know what would be more meaningful to me throughout my day? If I took time to help someone who needed it, made someone smile, or connected with my kids.

Taking the time to insert something fulfilling into my day is moving me toward a goal of living with intent. To let go of the endless mental to-do list and notice what's going on around me. To actively let go of the constant busywork nonsense and take in what's happening in the now. Look out the window, let the sun soak in, get that tan (or burn) on, notice nature, be calm, grateful, and at peace for a moment in my crazy, nonstop day. To find a way to make my soul sing when I connect with another person, improve the community, or brighten someone's day. That's what I call winning.

One point that really hits home for me is that my children are learning from my actions that they're supposed to constantly be "busy." I'm not teaching them to live a life of value and intent if I'm always running around like a crazy person, trying to work from my phone, doing errands, cleaning, and stressing out about little things.

One of my biggest goals this year is to take time to be 100 percent devoted to just them each day, even if it's for a short period of time. To truly listen to what they're saying, to expose them to new experiences, and to show them that life isn't about getting everything done but rather being grateful for this incredible life we have. It is so taken for granted. That stops now!

Intent is who we aspire to be as individuals, family members, and in our community. Most of us don't realize it, but we're living life in the passenger seat, allowing moments to pass us by while we keep our head in a cloud of day-to-day busywork. Are you striving each day to be the person you aspire to be, or do you feel as though you're simply surviving?

Often times, by the end of the day, even though you've checked off the one million items on your mental checklist, you still feel frustrated, exhausted, and unsettled. Guess what? Tomorrow morning you'll get up and do it all over again. Yep, you're filling your day with tasks, but you're utterly unfulfilled, and your soul is hitting that snooze button.

Living your life with intention means actively taking control of moments throughout your day. Choosing how you want to exert your precious energy, what you will surround yourself with, who you will connect with, and the thoughts that will fill your head.

A great way to start moving in the right direction is to take some time to realize exactly what's important to you and the direction you hope your life will take in the future. Take a minute to do some daydreaming about your ideal life. If money weren't a struggle, what would you be doing with your life? Where would you live? Who would be in this life? What would you fill your days doing? What does health, happiness, and purpose mean for you? Stop and think about that. I'll be waiting right here. . . .

Now that you have some goals and direction, when a situation arises in your day, you can simply say, "Is this action getting me closer to my goals and ideal life?" If the answer is no, you can leave that bad juju behind and focus your energy on something that *moves* you. It's simple, right?

Think about what it means to live your day in each of the following ways.

When presented with the opportunity, which of these will you choose to live intently with?

Freedom or Guilt?

Risk or Mundane?

Love or Fear?

Action or Thought?

Giving or Taking?

Connection or Solitude?

Growth or Sedentary?

Amazing day or Every day?

Shoot for the unrealistic stars or Stay in your safe place?

Emit the glow of who you are for the world to soak up or Live in fear of other people's thoughts?

No matter what your goals and dreams are, large or small, soccer mom or CEO of that multibillion-dollar company, common or whacky, if you conquer your goals with conviction and passion, you'll be living with intent.

MIND YOUR MINDSET:

BRAIN GAMES

Living with intent begins with your mind. In recent years, science has done a complete 180 on how the brain works. Not too long ago it was believed that the brain you were born with is the brain you ended with. They thought each area had only one function, and the brain was a machine which could only work at a certain capacity. So basically, you're either born downright stupid or with the ability to do great things. I call BS.

Today, science has proven that we were way off base. The brain can be formed, changed, improved, and controlled. It doesn't simply have one function in each area as once believed, but each area can be used in multiple ways—even to control functions happening in our own body. We have much more control over our physical life than we once thought.

Think of the brain as a muscle. To get some killer biceps, you lift weights. One of the fastest ways to gain control over and shape your brain to maximize its benefits is meditation. I know, most of you just rolled your eyes and said, *"Yeah, I'm not sitting in a weird position on the floor with my eyes closed, trying to levitate."*

Guys, stop making it weird. Meditation is scientifically proven to have tons of health benefits in your life. It's like going to the gym for your brain. Simply put, meditation is gaining control over your mind.

Many people live their lives with their minds and thoughts controlling them, where it should be the other way around; it should be you having more control over your thoughts, feelings, and reactions, and that's exactly what meditation trains you to do. Once you're skilled at being in control of your own mind, you're able to focus more clearly for longer periods of time, control your emotional reactions to situations, and allow yourself to connect to your inner self to get a clear picture of your needs and desires.

Meditation is a basic practice. It's simply focusing your brain on one thing for longer than usual. Some folks like to focus on breathing as their stomach moves in and out, some choose a sound to focus on, such as a waterfall, some like to picture sun shining on them and into their body. It doesn't matter what you choose to focus on as much as keeping the focus continuous. The longer you can focus on this one thing, the more you're strengthening your mind and the control you have over it.

For beginners, start out nice and easy. Set a timer for just a few minutes if you're a newbie. Do your best not to allow other thoughts to pop in. Cough, did Meghan Markle and Prince Harry really just launch an Instagram for their baby? Oops, closing the app on my phone now. The point is, those thoughts will pop in, which is normal and okay, but bring yourself right back to focus. Sorry, royal baby, I'll have to check out your Instagram later. Sometimes thoughts that pop in during meditation are good insight into what's going on underneath the busy day-to-day business. So listen, then immediately refocus. You can think about the topics that popped in once you're done.

The more you improve in this practice, the longer you'll keep focus without the unruly thoughts popping in, and the more you'll be in control of your emotional responses, calmness, focus, and stamina throughout your day.

Further proof that meditation can change your brain and your lifestyle is documented in several recent studies on participants with ADD and ADHD. Both children and adults found immense improvements in their symptoms after regular mindfulness meditation practices. Dr. Lidia Zylowska (2008) executed a study showing 78 percent of participants who practiced mindful awareness reported reduction in their ADHD symptoms. If you're not a big fan of the many medications they offer for this disorder, meditation is a great place to start. They even have special guided meditations for folks with ADD/ADHD, and more specifically, children who suffer from it.

Improving the focus on your mind allows you to control the way you respond to basic events. For example, when stuck in traffic, many people jump to the reaction of frustration and anger that result in Hulk-like road rage. But what if you chose not to have a blood-boiling response? What if you chose to control your reaction and decide to find the positive in the situation? What if you directed your thoughts toward something along the lines of, "I get to take a moment to think in peace and quiet, to listen to my favorite song, or to settle my mind?" Your day won't be ruined, your stress and anxiety level will be down, and you can move forward in a confident way while jamming out to your favorite tunes. We don't need to waste our energy on unnecessary stress. We can't control the traffic. We can control how we choose to react, filling our body with either stress or happiness.

Our minds are always in a state of judging. And I'm not talking, "OMG, look at her outfit!" but rather is this situation good or bad, right or wrong, is it what I want or don't want? Controlling your mind gives you the power to stop judging and quiet your busy thoughts. Not everything needs to be labeled good or bad, and not everything needs to happen in a certain way.

Learning to react with positivity allows you to go with the flow and take everything that life throws at you in stride. You lose the need to control situations, seek outside approval, and depend on *outside* objects for *internal* happiness. Try committing a day, or even just a few hours, living without judgment of the day's moments. Allow the day's events to happen freely without your busy mind making constant decisions on where each moment stands in your judgments.

MIND YOUR MINDSET:

EGO AND FIXED MINDSET

VS.

TRUE SELF AND GROWTH

MINDSET

When I say ego, most people think of a big jock unnecessarily strutting his stuff because he thinks he's God's gift to the world. Dude, you're not, so stop with the flexing. That type of ego isn't cool either, but I'm talking about the *Ego Self.* To simplify this, let's break it into two categories: True Self and Ego Self.

Your Ego Self is like a mask you wear over your True Self. Your Ego Self is basing your happiness and decisions on outside factors like the approval of others, power, and material objects. In this mindset you always desire to be in control in order to react to these outside situations. You're disinterested in a task if you're not immediately skilled and successful at it. This is also widely known as a Fixed Mindset.

When you are in Ego Self, it is a dangerous source of happiness. You base everything on outside factors. This is a slippery slope because things like cars, promotion, and external power can be taken away at any time.

Your True Self, on the other hand, is calm. It's immune to criticism, judgment, and status. You don't react to outside situations but rather choose how events will proceed. You are humble, kind, and open. You are eager to accept challenges, value education, and strive for personal growth. Aka, Growth Mindset.

So how does this work into your own life? I was listening to an interesting training from my favorite motivational speaker, business guru, and fellow MA native, Katie Wood. She spoke about preparing to go on stage to speak, and like any first-time speaker standing in front of hundreds of faces, she was so nervous about the process that she thought she might literally vomit. She started pounding grapes in hopes that they'd somehow turn to wine after consumption to calm her nerves (before you get too excited, that doesn't actually work).

Katie asked fellow event speaker and businesswoman extraordinaire, Kat Cole, how she remained so calm before she went live, and her answer was simple: "ego." Prior to going live, Katie was in a mindset of allowing her Ego Self to call the shots. She was concerned with outside validation, how she would look, and whether she would be successful. The host told her to drop that ego like a bad habit, because, well, it is one.

If what Katie had to say could help just one person, then her time there was a success. Her True Self focused on the one and only goal of helping another to hear information that may shift their mindset and better their life. This message gave her the calmness and confidence to go out there and say what she needed to say while losing the fear of judgment and failure.

In another scenario a student is standing in front of the class for a presentation. I was always the kid who would sweat through the whole class and just before it was my turn, I'd pull something like, *"There's a puppy and a baby headed toward a burning building! They're in serious danger; I better go help!"* then swiftly exit the classroom and flee to Taco Bell. I know. So relatable, right?

On the flip side, if I had been living with a True Self or Growth Mindset, I would've been eager to present and learn from the professor on how to improve because that is in fact the whole point of education. If I had said something incorrect, I'd simply have been corrected, and therefore would have grown from the experience.

If you have fears, guilt, or insecurity over subjects such as money, objects, or judgment, then it's true that basic aspects of your personality are fear, guilt, and insecurity. You won't be able to fix these harmful traits by achieving the "success" an Ego Self would typically aim for—that shiny new car, power, or a raise. Those underlying personality traits will always remain in you until you connect with your True Self to gain control over and improve on those areas of negative reactions such as fear of judgment, guilt about yourself, or insecurity about money or tangible objects.

Next time you're in a challenging situation, ask yourself if you're responding as Ego Self or True Self and how you can transform that challenge into an opportunity. If someone pulls up in an amazing $100k car, is your reaction, "That's a beautiful car, congrats on your new purchase, how exciting!" or "Damn, I hope they don't look at my embarrassing car, I wish I had that expensive car, if I just had that car my life would be great." Ego self vs. True Self: one leaves you unfulfilled and loaded with stress, while the other leaves you with gratitude and fulfillment.

MIND YOUR MINDSET: Your Ticket to Success

"A stumbling block for the pessimist is a steppingstone for the optimist."

—*Eleanor Roosevelt*

A negative mind will never give you a positive life. That we know for certain. Do you ever notice that some people seem to shine wherever they go, draw people in, excel in activities they attempt, crush it in the professional world? That's not luck, honey.

Think about the most successful, influential people across the world. What do all of them have in common? A positive personal mindset. To successfully accomplish lofty goals, a person must first feel self-empowered and capable of achieving it through growth. This requires a positive mindset. In fact, there are a slew of celebs who often talk openly on how their success is owed to a basic positive mindset (to name a few: Denzel Washington, Jim Carrey, Oprah Winfrey, Jennifer Lopez).

Internal thoughts are what drives self-esteem, which informs us on how we perceive our self-worth—positively or negatively. Positive mindset allows you to disregard any outside nonsense, such as judgment from peers or preconceived limits. Their thoughts have zero effect on what you can and will accomplish. If you want to accomplish a feat outside of your norm, you will need to rely on your own positive mindset to find the drive to accomplish those goals, despite outside influences. Those with a positive mindset don't waste time complaining about their circumstances, but instead work with conviction to improve them.

The great thing about this extremely powerful gift of mindset is that you are 100 percent in control of what you feed your brain. Choose to empower yourself, celebrate your confidence, revel in your hard work, choose happiness, be grateful, and expect to accomplish great things.

You can literally change the outcome of a situation with your own personal mind power. Many people don't realize this incredible tool with which they're equipped. Now, before you begin to think I've gone looney talking about *mind control*, let's get our science on. Because as Bill Nye would say, science rules!

We all know about the placebo effect. Time and time again, doctors give half the patients the real medication and the other half a placebo. Almost every time, there are patients in the placebo group who begin to recover and fight the illness at elevated rates. Doctors attribute this to each patients' mental capacity to change their way of thinking, thus actually willing their body to react to and change its physical processes.

This even occurs with surgery. In a study delving into the power of positive mindset, Dr. Bruce Moseley (2002) of the Baylor School of Medicine gave half of the patients a knee replacement surgery and the other half had a placebo surgery. They literally sliced open a knee and did nothing. Yowzah.

Do you want to guess what happened? Patients in the placebo surgery began to recover at similar rates to the patients who had the actual surgery, due to changes made only in their mindset. The patients believed they had the surgery, and thus their mind was focused on the healing of their body. The change in the way they thought about their injury and their body's ability to heal allowed them to shift into a healing cycle from within.

This mindset theory carries across the board and can be applied to your success in life, business, and finances. The key is utilizing this "super power" of controlling our minds to create change in our life. Our mind holds much more power than most of us realize, and it's willing and able to help us succeed when we're ready to put it to use.

Have you heard of the 40-percent rule? The Navy Seals have a theory on mindset: The average brain tells you to tap out at about 40 percent of exertion. That means you still have a reserve tank of energy and willpower waiting to be accessed by your mind. *We're conditioned to only do as much we've been able to do in our past experiences.* The reality is if you choose to mentally push through and continue, you will realize your reserve tank is on standby, ready to help you complete your goal. I'm not saying you can become Superman if you try hard enough, but if you're looking to complete that long-distance run, break that bad habit, stay on that healthy eating plan, increase your patience, or finish that book you've been working on for years, challenge yourself to use your mind to break into that reserve tank, go harder and longer than ever before, and change the physical outcome.

MIND YOUR MINDSET: ENERGY, FREQUENCY, VIBRATION, GOD, PANCAKES, KARMA

I know what you're thinking. What in the hot hell do all of the things listed above have in common? Also, now I'm hungry for pancakes, so thanks for that, Ali. Sorry about making you hungry, but I promise it's relevant.

There are many religions, many gods, many studies, and many beliefs on what makes this universe tick. This tends to be a sensitive topic for many, so let me tiptoe through the tulips with you for a moment while we explore some thoughts.

Folks can be spiritual, scientific, or religious, and although everyone has their own strong beliefs on this topic, I personally believe that most religions and beliefs are in place to achieve the same goals: to encourage us to live a better life, to be of value to our community, to help others (which inevitably leads to helping ourselves), and to understand that you do have the power to change your reality and make an impact by taking action.

No matter what you call the driving force behind this great universe—source energy, God, cosmic energy, higher power, intuition, karma, pancakes—it's important to realize that everything is connected, and we have the ability to harness this power to change our lives in a positive way. If this feels questionable to you, ponder this: we live on a *blue* planet that circles around a *ball of fire*, next to a moon that *moves the sea*. Mind. Blown. Allow yourself to believe that some amazing things are happening out there and roll with it!

To simplify things, positive actions, like helping others, make us feel good inside. This results in positive things happening to us, *and* there's a reason for this.

Let's vibe out, scientifically speaking.

You've probably heard the phrases, raise your vibration, I'm getting good vibes, or even The Beach Boy's hit song, "Good Vibrations." It may be hard to believe, but everything on this planet and beyond holds a certain vibration. The universe started out as a ball of energy, and it's important to realize that you are not separate from this energy. You are made of, have control over, and can harness this very energy.

Certain vibrations (high or low) attract like-vibrations. This is called the law of attraction. Learn it, live it, love it, because it's about to get you to the promised land, so to speak (which the tulip garden clarifies can mean anything from the career you desire, happiness you crave, or the place of your choosing after life). The principles of the law of attraction go as far back as 391 BC and are the basis of many studies today.

When we talk about "raising your vibration," we're talking about literally vibrating at a higher speed. Love, hope, compassion, and kindness are all emotions that vibrate at a very high speed. Greed, fear, hate, and sadness vibrate at lower speeds. Everything you desire and don't desire is vibrating at a frequency. This gives you the power to attract what you want and to distance yourself from what you don't.

The way in which we spread good attitudes toward other people and attract kindness, generosity, and success can be partly explained with reference to mirror neurons—neurons that "mirror" the behavior we observe. In other words, when someone sees you radiating positivity, this same response is mirrored in the brain of the observer. This can draw them to act positively toward you as well. Meanwhile, studies on the amygdala (the brain's emotional center) show that we induce feelings of fear and anxiety in others if we ourselves are fearful or anxious. This is further evidence to explain the law of attraction theorist's claim that negative thinking can prevent success, well-being, love, and human connection.

Although philosophers have been talking about this for as long as we know, Dr. Masaru Emoto (2008) released his study examining the effects of the vibrations of our words. By simply repeating a word or phrase to water, he claims that positive words created crystals of a higher vibration. Negative words created crystals that looked like a result of being subjected to lower vibrations of energy. The words being said repeatedly (thank you, mean phrases, positive prayer) changed the shape of the crystals, supporting the different levels of vibration within our words.

Many studies have been conducted on music as well. Songs that carry a negative message also emit lower vibrations, which in turn make you feel negative. So choose your playlist wisely! Since ancient times, music and sound have been used in a medical capacity for healing. Today, studies have found that listening to music you enjoy with high vibrations may increase the release of pleasure-causing substances in the brain like norepinephrine, melatonin, and dopamine (Blood and Zatorre, 2001). As a result, music therapy has the power to reduce stress/ease anxiety, improve sleep, lessen a depressed mood, create a positive mood, boost self-confidence, and increase energy. Listening to music seems to be able to change brain functioning to the same extent as medication. Since music is so widely available and inexpensive, it's an easy, stress-reducing option (Haas and Brandes, 2006).

Fun Fact: Which types of music helps in stress reduction most efficiently?

- Native American, Celtic, Indian stringed-instruments, drums and flutes

- Sounds of rain, thunder and nature sounds

- Light jazz, classical and easy listening music

Alright, time to get Godly.

Religion offers many benefits across the board, but right now, we're just taking a look at how it relates specifically to the *positive energy that allows us to harness change* in our current life.

Science and religion are often at odds, but in reality, when it comes to positivity, they're greatly connected. Prayer is scientifically proven to raise your vibrations, aka to make you feel better, as seen in Dr. Emoto's studies. That's something we can all get on board with.

Additionally, there is a large body of research on the health, economic, and educational benefits of religion. Most researchers have found that these specific benefits of religion are related to *regular religious attendance*.

Meaning it's less about the strength of your faith and more about the dependability of your arrival at religious services and events. Listening to the positive "high vibration" messages on a regular basis has many benefits.

Please join me back in the tulip garden for a side note: All the results presented here are benefits found to derive from religious attendance or involvement in any religion, so there is nothing here to suggest that one's particular beliefs are the key to the results. It is having the beliefs, practicing them, and regularly joining with other like-minded adherents that produce the benefits reported here.

Check out some of the statistically proven benefits of regular religious involvement. People who attended regularly exhibited a stronger immune system, lower blood pressure, less depression, less alcohol and drug use, less juvenile delinquency, better school attendance, and a higher probability of graduating from high school.

"Most religions emphasize love of others, compassion, and altruistic acts, as well as encourage meeting together during religious social events. These prosocial behaviors have many consequences that buffer stress and lead to human support when support is needed during difficult times. Because religion encourages the helping of others and emphasizes a focus outside of the

self, engagement in other-helping activities may increase positive emotions and serve to distract from one's own problems. Religion also promotes human virtues such as honesty, forgiveness, gratefulness, patience, and dependability, which help to maintain and enhance social relationships. The practice of these human virtues may also directly increase positive emotions and neutralize negative ones." (Koenig, 2012)

So if religion is your thing, raising your vibrations with consistent prayer, positive messages, and True Self behaviors is another way to better your life and attract the things to move you closer to your dream life.

"Whatever a Man Is Sowing, This He Will Also Reap."

—Gal. 6:7, 8.

In the end, whether you're into science, religion, spirituality, or pancakes, whatever you're throwing down is what you'll be picking up. Act accordingly.

MIND YOUR MINDSET:

STRESS, ANXIETY, AND FEAR,

OH MY!

Anxiety is one of the most common illnesses in America today. Rather than load up on meds, people are harnessing the power of mindset control, which in turn, dictates how their bodies will react to any given situation, aka, anxiety vs. ease.

Step back into my science lab with me. When you hold a negative thought in your mind, it causes a physical reaction in your body, which releases cortisol, the stress hormone. That in turn, causes stress, elevated blood pressure, and anxiety. It's like a venom coursing through your body.

This being said, it's not the actual event that is causing the anxiety. It's the negative thoughts being held in your mind. The longer you hold on to those negative thoughts, the more cortisol continues release into your body, causing your blood pressure to rise and sending your body into a state of anxiety-ridden panic.

Before you start panicking about panicking, I've got good news: it is very much *in your control.* What if you decided to release those negative thoughts the second they entered your brain? This is something that takes practice, but man, is it freeing once you realize you do have control over your personal stress level.

One way to practice doing this is to have a few go-to responses to everyday situations that seem to be stress triggers.

For example, you've just opened your eyes and haven't even had a chance to sit up before the kids are bounding into you room, needing a hundred different things from you.

I might be drawing from personal experience, here. The point is, this is a big one for me because I tend to be a little, ahem, temperamental before the golden cup of joe. I usually say something like, *"Go watch TV until I make my coffee and your breakfast,"* trying desperately to not show my blood-boiling aggravation. That works about 10 percent of the time. *Dude! Can a girl get a second to open her eyes and run to the bathroom? Damn!*

Sorry, I got myself worked up for minute. I'll give you another scenario. What if I actively decided to release those negative feelings as quickly as they came on (yes, I do have that capability with some willpower and practice) and replace those thoughts of anxiety with a go-to response such as, "I'm happy my kids are so excited to see me. They think I'm an amazing mom who can provide all these things for them. They're healthy enough to come running into my room full of energy. I'm going to be the mom these happy kids deserve today."

Try waking up every morning and forcing your mind to have positive thoughts about yourself and your life. Choose to part ways with that stress hormone you're way too familiar with. Bye, Felicia.

Instead, send those happy endorphins coursing through your now energized body. Choose to smile, embrace the chaos, and watch your morning routine change in the most magnificent way, even without that cup of coffee.

MIND YOUR MINDSET:

LITTLE MINDS

What your children believe about themselves is what they will, in turn, become. If you have the ability to make them believe they're strong, smart, happy, amazing, and capable, why not give them that advantage in life?

So let's talk children. Maybe you have kids, maybe you want them someday, maybe you hate those crazy little gremlins because they're loud in restaurants and a hot mess of filth and chaos (I mean, all of that IS true), but you do have a best friend with children who could use this advice—and let me tell you, she needs all the help she can get. We all do. Right now, I'm holding up the *Hunger Games* sign high in the air to all the mommas out there in the struggle.

Either way, you should find this info useful at some point in your everchanging life.

It's human nature to dwell on negative thoughts more so than the positives. Children don't know they can grow certain parts of their brain with practice, which is why it's your job to give them a step up in life and cultivate a positive mindset in them right from the beginning.

Remember how those super successful people all had positive mindsets which helped catapult them to accomplishing their wildest dreams? Imagine if you could set up your child (or friend's gremlin child) with a head start for success and happiness right from the beginning?

A study by Lang Chen (2012) proves having a positive attitude acts directly on your memory and learning system. "Based on our data, the unique contribution of positive attitude to math achievement is as large as the contribution from IQ." Teaching positive mindsets can help your child excel in the classroom and beyond. Easy enough, let's do it!

There are many ways you can give children a head start, but first, I think it's important to note that children have a whole range of emotions, and it's important for them to feel all of them. If something negative happens, it's important for them to still feel the negative emotions and process them. The key is teaching them how to process these thoughts and situations in that healthy way.

So let's get to it. Positive thinking broadens children's sense of possibility, opens their mind, increases confidence, and makes them more resilient both in minor day-to-day situations, as well as major life adjustments.

Your brain can be trained to be more emotionally resilient and to respond to certain emotions in a healthier manner. This is done by consistently working certain thoughts and actions into your child's daily routine in a fun and engaging way. It should never feel like "work" for them to be positive, rather a normal part of their life.

We have a morning chore chart at home. Yeah, go ahead and laugh; I know I did when I saw another mom bragging about hers on Facebook. But you guys, this thing is nothing short of life changing for my hectic mornings! It has all the usual tasks (clear breakfast dishes, teeth, face, dress, etc.) but at the end it says, "look in the mirror and give yourself a compliment." They love the feeling of accomplishment after completing each step and then running to the mirror to say something great about themselves. It's fun for me to watch—turns out three-year-olds come up with some pretty hilarious "compliments"—and it makes my soul sing to see their smiling, confident faces before they head off to tackle the day at school.

Kind of like with meditation, a lot of people think positive affirmations must be some new-age, cult-like activity where you stare deep into the mirror and whisper twenty sweet nothings to yourself.

Please don't be that person. This doesn't have to be weird. You can wake up in the morning and say a few things you're grateful for, things you hope will happen, or a certain way you want to act. Remember, for me it's saying something like, "I'm the great mom that these happy kids deserve."

Right now, I'm lucky enough to live on the water, so when I sit up and see the waves, I think about how grateful I am for the house we have, my ability to work hard to obtain it, and my healthy family who lives in it. Sounds like a pretty easy way to start filling your body with those happy hormones, right? Well, the same goes for children.

As I mentioned earlier, it's human nature for your thoughts to dwell on the negatives. Therefore, at the end of each day (we do it at the dinner table), it's helpful to talk about a few positive moments that happened throughout your day. Seeing you talk about some positives will guide them to realize some of their own.

When we first started this, most of the kids' positives involved food or playing. Hey, Cal loves his food and dump trucks, and I get it, they're both very cool. But as we've progressed a bit, I'm hearing comments such as, "Someone shared a toy with me, and it was really nice." This seemingly small shift is important because it's helping them to realize and enjoy the small positives happening in their day and to be grateful for the little but awesome moments they're experiencing. They're realizing how an act of kindness made both parties feel: happy.

Hearing that the high point of my daughter's day was helping someone who was feeling sad at school is enough to A) make my heart explode and B) give me the motivation to continue putting in the effort to cultivate positive mindsets.

Goal setting is another point of attack when boosting up mindset. As you can imagine, learning to set and obtain goals is very important for children. The simple task helps them to gain independence, develop motivation, grow a sense of purpose, improve focus, and realize they do in fact have control over their life's outcomes. Aka, a positive mindset. What better way to set your child up for a successful future?

When your child decides on their own goals to achieve, they become driven for their own personal satisfaction, rather than to please others or to acquire tangible rewards.

Studies show children who created and accomplished goals from a young age (sports, academic, personal), had significantly higher levels of achievement compared to those who didn't have meaningful goals. Also, children who witnessed the success of their own goals had the highest levels of self-worth and self-efficacy (Bogolin, Harris, and Norris, 2003).

Once you come up with a list of fun, attainable, short-term goals, help your kids (er, or friend's kids) break it down into what steps will help them achieve it.

Nowadays there are a multitude of resources to help guide both you and the child through positive practices like these. There are apps for children's meditation, affirmations, and even goal setting. What a world we live in!

MIND YOUR MINDSET:

KEEP YOUR HEAD, HEELS, AND

SELF-WORTH HIGH

If she's strong, she's a bitch.

If she demands more in her partner, she's crazy.

If she works hard for her success, she got lucky.

If she knows her worth, she's conceited.

If she displays her intelligence, she's egotistical.

But this woman isn't about to give up on her potential or settle for an ounce less than she deserves.

She hears these names and gracefully persists on her journey to become the woman aspires to be.

— #PrettyCombat

Know your self-worth. Then add tax. Self-worth is a big one around these parts. I work my ass off to be the magnificent, kind, hardworking, respectful, positive ray of freaking sunshine that I am, and I deserve that in return. Plus tax.

The way you see yourself is a major factor in the decisions you make, and therefore, the life you create. It dictates how well you take care of yourself, the quality of people you surround yourself with, who you choose as a partner, your level of persistence and resilience, and the chances you decide to take to move toward your goals.

Ya'll, I'm not saying to go out there and be a cocky asshole to the world, but it's crucial that you believe in yourself and give yourself a chance to step outside of your current situation and achieve things *greater than your present.*

It's also important to realize that self-worth is not something to be compared to another person. You do not need to be better than others in any certain area to feel accomplished, happy, proud, and worthy. I think in this current social media-obsessed world it's easy to get lost in subconsciously comparing your life to the photoshopped lives of others on social media.

There will always be someone who appears wealthier, prettier, happier, stronger, funnier, etc., so we end up fighting a losing battle. I promise that Deborah doesn't have the perfect hair, nails, clothes, and family she posts about daily. You all have a Deborah in your life. Ignore her. Instead, we should focus on our own personal values and accomplishments within.

Not only is it a losing battle to compare these things, but it's actually unhealthy. One study at the University of Michigan found that college students who base their self-worth on external sources (academic performance, appearance, and approval from others) reported more stress, anger, academic problems, and relationship conflicts. They also had higher levels of alcohol and drug use, as well as more symptoms of eating disorders. The same study found that students who based their self-worth on internal sources not only felt better, they also received higher grades and were less likely to use drugs and alcohol or to develop eating disorders (Crocker, 2002).

So although social media is quite entertaining, nix the self-comparisons as you scroll.

Our own *inner critic* is another detriment to our self-worth. We're hard wired to examine the negatives about ourselves, which can be exhausting and damaging. You complete a task (good job!), but immediately your inner critic starts examining it, saying thing like, *Is that part good enough? It doesn't look like Suzie's version. What are others going to think? Did I make a bad choice? I should have finished yesterday.*

Do you ever try to fall asleep, and your inner critic starts thinking about all the stupid things you did years ago? Yeah, that tequila/rum/vodka night was a bad idea, but it does nothing for you to rehash past mortifications and shortcomings.

The good news is you can challenge that inner critic, punch it right in the face, and tell it how freaking awesome you are. Examining our negatives is unhealthy and ineffective. It's a big ol' waste of time. As we know (because I've pounded it into your head one hundred times), you can rewire and retrain your brain to see your value, move on to the next task, and knock it out of the park. You are in control of your mind.

This route allows you to keep that forward motion and continue to improve while seeing the badass warrior you really are. It's important to take control of your thoughts rather than allow them to "happen to you." If you fail to stand guard at the door of your mind, then you are giving access to delusional and disenchanting thoughts, sending you backward. Your mind is a beautiful fortress; you decide what's allowed inside the gate.

"Your self-worth is determined by you. No outside person, circumstance or situation can affect that. If you're consistently trying to prove your worth to someone, you've already forgotten your value." — #PrettyCombat

MIND YOUR MINDSET:

RELEASING THE GUILT

We've been pre-conditioned to find guilt everywhere in our day to day. Whether it's our bodies, our parenting, our friendships, or our lifestyle, it's in our faces.

Today's world of social media and online platforms are filled with "informative" posts, which can be written by anyone, and everyone seems to have an opinion. Unfortunately, many of those people don't have a great understanding of the fact that each person's life is, wait for it, *different!* One of the biggest and most difficult tasks as a human is to unlearn what you've been told to feel guilty about.

Some people are more prone to put shame and guilt on themselves. This is something that has been conditioned throughout life, rather than a limitation some were born with. This is a great thing because if it's been conditioned, it can also be reversed. The good news is, guilt is 100 percent constructed in your mind. That same mind we've learned that *we* have control over through practice.

One of the biggest guilts out there is about your body. No matter what the shape, size, body-fat percentage, your body is an incredible machine. It can literally create human life and continue to feed and nourish it through survival. That should be enough, but check this out:

—Your stomach acid can dissolve metal.

—Your eyes can distinguish between 2.3 and 7.5 million different colors.

—When we touch something, the signal travels through the nerves to our brain at a speed of 124 mph.

—If the amount of water in your body decreases by 1 percent, you'll feel thirsty.

—At a rate of twenty million billion calculations per second, your brain makes world-class computers look as technologically advanced as a drinking bird.

—Our nose is our personal air-conditioning system: it warms cold air, cools hot air, and filters impurities.

—Approximately fifty thousand cells in your body will die and be replaced with new cells during the time it takes you to read this sentence. We make a new skeleton every three months and a new layer of skin every month.

—The skin is the body's largest organ, but it's also a pretty big medicine cabinet. The skin secretes antibacterial substances and serves as the first layer of defense for invading microorganisms. Most bacteria that land on the skin die quickly.

Okay, enough with the random body facts, but you get my point. Your body is absolutely freaking incredible, no matter what shape or size it is today. Be grateful for the body you have at this very moment and treat it well.

As if fretting about your body isn't enough, how about the guilt as a parent? It's the motherload of daily "holy shit, am I making the right decisions for this small human?" guilt trips. It all starts at their birth. Nope, scratch that, it all starts with the decision to even have a child or not.

You begin to have thoughts, lots of sweat-inducing thoughts:

Does my child need a sibling, or am I destining them for single-child boredom, am I too young/old, do I have enough income, have the right house, do I have enough time to give them, am I healthy enough, will I be a good parent? And the list goes on . . . and on . . . and on.

Once you commit, it switches to things like, am I eating the right foods, gaining too much weight, not gaining enough weight, choosing the right doctor, choosing the right birthing method, all while still thinking of the aforementioned guilty thoughts.

Once the child is born, hold onto your pants, folks, because it's about to go into guilt overload.

Breastfeeding? Formula? Co-sleeping? Cry it out method? Stay-at-home mom? Working mom? Daycare? Nanny? Sleeping position? Swaddle process? Homemade baby food? Organic everything? Let someone/something hold the bottle for a quick second? Let them sleep more/less? Clean the house more? Shower more? Cry less?

Once they get older, the list keeps coming. Getting into single parent territory . . . Don't even get me started.

Basically, either yourself or an outside factor will make you feel guilty about any decision you make. The only thing you can be truly confident in is that *no one can ever give more pure love to that child than you.* And that's the only thing that truly matters. That's the big one.

So what if we practiced removing our guilt for every little thing? What if none of this was *actually* a problem? What if it truly doesn't matter if everything your baby touches is 100-percent organic? What if the house not being 100-percent spotless is helping them build immunities to dust and germs (I'm sure if I looked, I could find some sort of study to back this up, but this is really just my own assessment to make me feel like I'm not failing)? What if it's equally hard AF to be a working mom and a stay-at-home mom? People can say whatever they please about that topic, but there are equal amounts of pros and cons for both situations, and only you know what's best for your family.

So let's start making our decisions with pride and confidence and practice *releasing* any guilt we start to feel creep in, which in turn fill our bodies with the stress hormone. No one will love your child more, have your motherly instinct, or know what's best for your child more than you. End of story. Summoning my Gandalf voice: guilt be gone.

Maybe you have a perfect body and no children (cheers to you!), but guilty situations are found across the board with friends, works, family, health, basically every part of your life. Practice releasing those thoughts and moving forward with conviction.

MIND YOUR MINDSET:

FILL THAT FREAKIN' CUP

TO THE BRIM

Let me paint a heavenly picture for you: A well-rested mom wakes up to her adorable children asking for the TV on, some milk, and a lovingly made breakfast of their choice. The mom springs out of bed and kindly gives her children everything they desire before helping herself to her own needs.

To that mom . . . take a hike. I mean, you're an amazing superhero, but that is not something I, or most people I know, can relate to. My kids are well aware that if shit goes down before I've made my coffee, they're in serious trouble, and my redheaded superpower of overreaction will be in full effect.

Stewardesses say it best. *"Before you assist others, always put on your own oxygen mask first."*

The same goes for that old "filled cup" analogy. You must first fill your own cup in order to serve others; you can't pour from an empty cup. You're not able to successfully help anyone else if you've not taken care of yourself first.

For me, it's about taking care of myself before I can be a great parent. Because raising little humans to be happy, respectful, and not complete assholes, is exhausting. And the pristinely clean house thing? Well, that's a work in progress. But this applies to everyone's job, relationships, friendships, and home life. If you're miserable, you're probably not an awesome friend to hang out with or a solid coworker, never mind actively helping others.

Work is a big concern within this topic. So many people live to work rather than work to live; however, our personal life should come before work. If you died (sorry, that's totally morbid) but your company would act to replace you within the day. It's understandable that you need to work to live, but never forget that your health and happiness is the priority for both you and any loved ones who depend on you.

Take my mom for example: she is one badass lady. She handles the load of a hundred men and does it all with a perfect outfit and a smile. She's the queen of pushing it down deep and pushing on. No matter how many curveballs life throws at her—and there have been a lot—she's always lovely and handling it without letting on that some big, difficult thing is happening. Until this winter.

Despite being a professional stress-hoarding ninja, her body simply couldn't handle it anymore. Years of putting everyone before herself, while not taking care of her body and mind, literally landed her in the hospital. Your body does have a limit to what it can take, so it's important to care for yourself now, rather than when it's too late. It's not selfish to take time to replenish your body, mind, and soul. It's vital to both your own health and to care for the people who need you most. No matter what life is throwing down, don't feel guilty about filling that freakin' cup, friend (with soda, wine, a splash of tequila—I'm not here to judge). Cheers.

Here are some ways to fill your cup (beyond coffee):

Treat yo'self—When you look good, you feel good. Get your hair done, put together some great outfits, do your nails, score a new accessory, grab some sunless tanner and pretend you've been somewhere exotic—whatever makes you feel like your most beautiful you. Hit reset on your appearance, and find the excitement in putting yourself first again.

Take a timeout—If you're busy 24/7, you're either taking on too much or really awful at time management (#sorrynotsorry). Choose to not please others for a minute and *just say no*. Anyone else having D.A.R.E flashbacks right now? But seriously, secure that golden time for yourself to refocus and recover. No tidying up, no thinking about work, no talking. Just be. Sip a special coffee, read a book, take a walk, enjoy the silence.

Find something that sets your soul on fire—Whether it's a hobby, a new skill, a passion business, or a sport, find something that excites you and make a point to adjust your schedule to fit it in on a regular basis.

Get up slightly earlier—Yeah, I love sleep too. But time for a wake-up call: there are a multitude of studies supporting the practice of waking up a bit earlier to make time for yourself. Meditation, exercise, and simply focusing on good things has proven time and time again to be majorly beneficial to your mind, body, and all-over happy vibes.

See friends—Yes, in person like people used to do back in the old days. No texting, messaging, or Snapchatting, if that's your thing. Real life, face-to-face interactions with people you'd actually *choose* to spend your time with. Connecting with another person is a proven way to uplift your day.

Side note: You don't have to do the whole *"I'm finally seeing my friend, let's get wasted and have a crazy night full of regrets and week-long hangovers."* Scheduling an hour for lunch and a chat could change the feel of your whole week ahead.

Go outside—Nature has a profound impact on our brains and our behavior. Connecting with nature soothes your soul on many levels. When folk's stress levels were examined after taking a daily walk of the same distance in a *forest* as opposed to an *urban* setting, it showed they exhibited much lower stress levels, lower heart rate, decreased anxiety, increased focus, increased creativity, and better over-all moods (Ewert & Chang, 2018).

In another experiment they studied the stress level of participants after watching a stress-provoking movie. The people, who were shown images of nature, recovered to their base levels at a much faster rate than those shown images of urban settings. Things like the repetitive motion of waves, sunshine, colors, and fresh air all contributed to soothing attributes of nature (Roger Ulrich, 2009).

Exercise—The science connecting exercise and confidence is extensive. Even if you work out one day, and your body doesn't actually look any different, your mindset will feel like a total badass. Obviously, how you feel on the outside connects with how you feel on the inside, but it's not about changing your appearance as much as switching it up and pumping your body full of endorphins while you sweat out the week's frustrations.

Listen to music—Music proven to change your mindset on the spot. Immediate gratification. So go download some strong, happy, high vibration music and blast that sh*t. When you're getting ready in the morning, driving to work, or cleaning up the house, rock on with your bad self.

Living space—Okay, so we don't all have the funds to redecorate our entire living area, but even sprucing up with a $5 pretty throw pillow, a candle, or a new house plant will change up the energy in your space and give you a little boost of excitement every time you walk into the room.

Before we take on Part 2 of this book, it's important to recognize that taking control over your mindset is imperative for creating a truly great life. Learn it, live it, love it. If you want to achieve all that you desire, the first step is getting your mind right—the next step? LEVELING UP.

PART 2–LEVEL UP

LEVEL UP: LEVEL UP AND GLOW

I can't say enough about the power of connecting with others. It opens doors left and right and presents you with opportunities you've most likely never entertained. Each person you meet is like a new trail opening off the beaten path—an opportunity filled with adventure and new sights, opening paths you've never dreamed of.

Personal connections are the main ingredient for a solid business. There are endless benefits to making true connections with others, rather than just cold networking. You'll find a deeper care and increased support in your business over competitors, honest feedback and tips on best practices, possibility to become partners or investors, creating access to things you once didn't have access to, such as events, locations, or other professionals, leads to new referrals, and lastly, a possible friendship and lifelong business-sounding board.

How about on a personal level? Those who have good relationships are happier, healthier, and live longer than those who report feeling lonely. As corny as it sounds, we as humans have a need to feel supported, valued, and loved—to be a part of something bigger than ourselves. Think about it: when you're moping around your house, feeling down and out, isn't it amazing how a simple conversation or phone call can turn your day around? We need connection to others in order to thrive. This doesn't have to be a tear jerking, heart to heart with someone close. Making a positive connection can be having a brief conversation with a neighbor on a walk, being kind to a store clerk, or going down to your local pub for a brew and a chat. Whichever way you choose, making a connection satisfies your inner need for community, something ingrained in us going back to the days of when cavemen were dependent on one another for survival.

You all know what that means? It's time to get our connection on! Have you ever noticed the woman who walks into the room and everyone turns to look as if they can feel her energy enter the area? You know her; she's the one whose smile shines happiness and comfort. The one who asks questions and makes eye contact because she genuinely cares about what you have to say.

People aren't noticing her because of her pretty face or nice clothes—it's the energy, confidence, and genuineness that she *chooses* to bring with her wherever she goes. It's not something she's born with, but rather how she chooses to look at life, connect, and live it with *intent.*

While it may take some practice to be the GLOW that enters the room and makes others feel engaged and comfortable, there are a few other little nuggets of info that could help bridge the gap.

It's been proven that when you approach another person with your hands visible and incorporated in your conversation, they immediately feel more at ease, trustful, and are more likely to befriend you. Not only does it help others' ability to connect with you, but it shows you're speaking with vulnerability, intent, and confidence (Gifford, Fan Ng, Wilkinson, 1985).

Think about meeting someone who has their hands hidden in their pockets vs. someone who shakes your hand and continues to show their hands throughout conversation. Pockets or crossed arms will show you're closed off, invulnerable to connecting, or just sketchy AF. Hands down by your sides is also closed and could even be portrayed as bored, uninterested, or conceited and confrontational. When you first meet someone, after a firm handshake (Keep your thumb straight up during handshakes. Turning their hand palm up forces your dominance, while showing your palms allows theirs.), try to gesture with your hands throughout rest of the conversation. Not like a crazy person, though. Keep it cool, man.

Eye contact is also a common and well-known strategy. We relate it to showing respect and confidence, however it has more benefits than you think. Eye contact actually produces a chemical called oxytocin, which makes us feel like we belong. Numerous studies have shown that people who make higher levels of eye contact with others are perceived as being more dominant and powerful, warm and personable, attractive and likable, qualified, skilled, competent, valuable, trustworthy, honest and sincere, confident, and emotionally stable (Kleinke, 1986; Hall et al., 2005). Say that ten times in a row. Side note: Don't stare into the other person's eyes without blinking for too long. There's a good chance they might think you're a serial killer if you do.

And let's not forget about the power stance—this is going to seem silly, but it's proven that when you widen your stance, your confidence skyrockets. A power stance is when you take up space, hold your arms and legs away from your body, straighten up, and keep your chin high. Go ahead and practice one; I swear you'll feel like you belong at the cool kid's table, and here's why: Harvard Business School professor Amy Cuddy explains, *"Body-mind approaches, such as power posing, rely on the body, which has a more primitive and direct link to the mind, to tell you you're confident."* She's talking about real confidence, like Kanye on Twitter, or really, Kanye anywhere. Cuddy continues to say, "When our body language is confident and open, other people respond in kind, unconsciously reinforcing not only their perception of us but also our perception of ourselves." So when you don't have time for the self-affirmations before that big conference call, step into a power pose and become the badass of the conversation.

Remember to show those pearly whites! But please, don't fake it. Assessing someone in the first few seconds is a basic skill of survival. If you approach someone with a fake smile, you'll immediately turn them off to an open connection with you. I know this is hard to do all of the time. None of us are happy every second of the day, but if it's important to you, find your inner happiness and channel your wishes to live with intent, and shine that smile that allows you to GLOW and connect.

Also, it's okay to be nervous. Those sweaty palms and pits (I know, pit stains are the worst) are an important reaction. I took a Sports Psychology course in college, where I learned that nerves are actually quite beneficial. They show that you care about something, prove that this is something you'd like to accel at, and validify that the task is something worth putting your energy into. Your body's reaction to nervousness is extremely close to the feelings of excitement. This means, before something like an event or meeting someone new, you can mentally claim nervousness as excitement for something important. Lean in to the excitement and make a night worth living!

"You will meet plenty of people who are pretty but haven't yet learned how to be beautiful. They will have the right look for the times but they will not glow. Beautiful women glow. When you are with a beautiful women you might not notice her hair or skin or body or clothes, because you'll be distracted by the way she makes you feel. She will be so full of beauty that you will feel some of it overflow onto you. You'll feel warm and safe and curious around her. Her eyes will twinkle a little and she'll look at you really closely, because beautiful wise women know that the quickest way to fill up with beauty is to soak in another human being. Women who are concerned with being pretty think about what they look like, but women who are concerned with being beautiful think about what they're looking at."

—*Glennon Doyle Melton, Love Warrior*

LEVEL UP: GETTING SMART ABOUT DOLLA DOLLA BILLS, Y'ALL

After spending ten years on the hamster wheel known as real estate, scraping by, and working what seemed like 24/7 for each and every paycheck—which was not guaranteed at any time—I decided to get smart with my extremely valuable personal time, study income and finance, and make a switch.

In this day and age, multiple streams of income are not only smart but crucial for many people. A solid side hustle is the new job security of today. Did you know the average millionaire has seven streams of income?

That means we need to get our diversifying on.

The great thing about sourcing a second income is you can focus your vehicle for revenue on something you're truly passionate about. When trying to live within your means, there's a limit to how much you can cut back on spending (you need heat, food, and shelter); however, there is no limit to how much you can earn. That's why instead of trimming expenses to boost the bottom line, I personally choose to increase earning. That's right, you can have that Grande Mocha Frappuccino Light *and* pay for gas. It's a win-win.

Your streams of income shouldn't be identical. Think about stocks: it's important to build a diversified portfolio to reduce risk. If you would diversify your investments, why wouldn't you do the same with your sources of income?

It not only works as a great safety net in the case of a lost job, but to live within your means, you either need to cut back on spending or make more money. You guys, I want that new pair of shoes to strut around town in . . . and the matching handbag . . . okay, *and* the new outfit to pull it all together. Should I be spending on that? Nope. But hey, a second or third avenue of income allows me to have that tasty looking slice of cake and eat it too.

But Ali, you may say, I can't spend all my time working! I need a life; I need that Wine Wednesday. Right you are (who doesn't need a Wine Wednesday?). There are only twenty-four hours in day, not all of which should be spent working. This is where the power of residual income comes in. Some businesses allow you to earn money over time while you're not actually physically working.

Once your business is up and running, you can lighten up on the workload and even use some of that income to create a new stream of income. It's a beautiful snowball effect that will get you into some killer shoes, on that vacation, or into that new home of your very own. The first venture will be your hardest, but each following venture will become easier with experience and will begin to build off of one another. There are many ways to earn passive income, but you'll need to think outside the box. For example, to keep it simple, say you invest in a vending machine. Even though you only have to tend to said vending machine once a week, it's making money for you all week long. You can focus your time on other things while bumping up your income and your lifestyle.

There are companies out there who allow you to start your own business using their products. Some are great, some are questionable. I won't name any names because who knows how companies will change over time, but if you're curious about the company I used to switch from a full-time job to a passion career, hit me up on our site or social media, and I'll give you my thoughts directly.

Another reason multiple streams of income are so valuable to me is because when I wake up in the morning, I can choose what I want to tend to that day. Although I work my ass off day in, day out, early morning, late nights, the flexibility of my work schedule makes it oh-so-worth-it to me.

It's important to know that not all businesses soar. You may have some that are failures, but you must risk to find the reward. Failure isn't fatal, but failure to try again, this time more intelligently, certainly is. You get your tough, scrappy ass up and work 'til you succeed. Don't worry about what others may think from the outside because you are the one bettering yourself and your family's lives while others dwindle away from their seat on the couch. You have a lot more coming to you in this life, and you're going to get up and get it.

LEVEL UP: LIFESTYLE UPGRADE

Don't underestimate the girl living on coffee and her dream.

Behind her sweet smile she has the fire and tenacity to make the impossible her reality.

Behind her womanly body, the strength to put full-grown men in their place if they doubt her leadership, abilities, or knowledge.

Behind her cute outfit and killer shoes is the insatiable drive to stay consistent with her hustle—while others are out galivanting—until she proves every last person wrong.

If you see this girl, don't doubt her. You'll want to be on her team down the road.

— #PrettyCombat

At some point, you decide you're sick of the struggle and get serious about creating a life you absolutely love. I wasn't born with "mommy and daddy money," I was born with "if I don't hustle, I'll have no money." I'm not meant for a life of living paycheck to paycheck or depending on another person to help me survive; the only person who can change that scenario is myself. It's amazing to be a woman who knows what she wants, but it's a whole different story to be the woman who's actively making that happen for herself. Let's all go be that woman, shall we?

No one is completely stuck where they are. Think you are? Send me a message, and I'll show you how to escape. I've made the great escape firsthand. So get up, power up, and become the CEO that your parents always wanted you to marry. Wave bye to Cinderella. *Your* story doesn't involve a prince saving the day. Get a plan, get a little (or a lot) savage, and give yourself permission to step out of the small and mundane and step into the big life—you're meant for greater things. Give yourself permission to think, build, and succeed big.

When making dreams come true from the ground up, belief is an invaluable ingredient for success: belief in yourself, belief that your opportunities are truly limitless, belief that you have the grit and fire inside to prevail.

You must become a badass woman with more faith than fear. One thing you'll find on your journey to success is your circle of people may change. This is okay. Not everyone is on the same plan as you, and the folks unworthy of your goals and dreams will fall by the wayside. But never apologize for being what someone else is not used to. Their thoughts, words, and actions have zero impact on your goals and journey to get to your pot of gold at the end of the rainbow.

Once you realize your own self-worth, there's a shift in energy. You start attracting people who respect your worth. You learn to surround yourself with people who force you to level up.

Keep in mind, those you surround yourself with are a great indicator of your future. Think about it: to accomplish your dreams, should you surround yourself with negative friends who go out and get drunk every night or surround yourself with the dreamers and doers who are actively motivated to better their lives and the lives around them? You know the answer. It doesn't mean you have to go out and be a dick to anyone, but if they're bringing you down, then they're not getting you closer to your own magnificent endgame. If you want to be successful, you have to be willing to disappear for a while, because success looks incredibly easy from the outside, but on the inside it's a head-down, consistent, relentless hustle. Almost every "overnight success" that you've heard of actually had years of hard work leading up to it. That hard work simply wasn't known to the world.

The same goes for a partner in your life. If the person you're so invested in isn't asking about your goals, dreams, and business, then girl, move on and reconsider all that energy you're investing in them. It's easy to find someone to Netflix and chill with, but it's hard to find someone to Netflix and *build* with. Sure, you two will binge watch *The Making of a Murderer*, but you'll also be building your empire and having a support system behind you while you do it.

Although becoming a leader means leaving a few of the negative, unworthy stragglers behind, the beautiful thing about a true leader is they empower and lift others with like mindsets to become leaders themselves. We build each other up. There's enough success and happiness to go around. Your competition isn't other people; it's how hard you'll work to crush your goals, how positively you'll react to situations thrown at you, and how healthy you'll treat your own body and mind. Compete against that.

When you find your passion and drive to conquer your dreams, there's nothing more empowering. It's feeling like sleep is now an inconvenience because you want to be awake, working on your real-life dream. It's talking about your plans with genuine passion, excitement, and certainty. It's feeling the rush of completing a goal, bringing you one step closer to your well-earned endgame. It's the feeling of truly living your life with value and intent because you're fully investing yourself in something meaningful to you. It's being more excited to show up Monday than to head home on Friday. It's feeling like a complete badass who's going to have a new, upgraded life when this is finished, with the hard work and battle scars to prove how you got there. Passion and desire drive success. Those who achieve success can't always say, *"I was successful because I was smarter than the average person."* But they will certainly say, *"I was unwaveringly passionate about this which cultivated my intense drive to achieve success."*

Life is a continuously transforming flow. People, things, and jobs come and go, but your education, self-worth, grit, and personal success will never leave you. It will be yours to have and to hold from this day forward. Now there's a vow that you can actually depend on, so go ahead and fall head over heels for the truly magnificent improvements in yourself.

Surround yourself with the dreamers and the doers. The ones who refuse to conform because their fire inside says they were born for more. The ones who have been bruised and broken and returned stronger than ever. The risk takers, rebels, and radiant souls. The thirsty hearts who refuse to settle for anything less than genuine. The untamed, wild-hearted, barefoot souls who sit in the moonlight, soaking in life's marvels while dreaming up their next adventure.

— #PrettyCombat

LEVEL UP: LIFT UP

While we're on the topic of surrounding yourself with solid people and lifting them up, what's up with the females who attempt to tear down? In this Kardashian age we're living in, it seems like frenemies are becoming more and more common. The worst is targeting someone who's trying to better their life and their family's lives by working hard. There's so much opportunity and success to go around. There's enough for everyone, and personally I find no greater joy than to lift someone up and help them get a taste of the glory. Let's bring it back to the social level. Can you think of an acquaintance who quite clearly tries to shut down other women she comes in contact with? I believe they think it will make them look better to others, but in reality, it's quite unattractive to be the one not lifting another woman up.

I highly doubt the type of person reading this book is also the type of person to tear another down, but just in case, picture this: One girl approaches a female with snarky comments, eye rolls, and insults, while the other says, *"It's great to meet you. You have such beautiful hair"* with a friendly smile. Nine times out of ten, people will choose to align with the girl exhibiting poise, kindness, and confidence. And that one person who doesn't choose that . . . oh, don't worry about that little guy . . . he's not on your level, and you should Roadrunner-style sprint as far away as possible.

When someone smiles at us, we naturally smile back; when someone is in pain, our bodies also reflect that emotion and physical sensation. Our wiring for empathy is so deep that just by observing someone else in pain, the "pain matrix" in our brain is activated.

Believe it or not, part of our survival instinct is to help each other. Society, jealousy, insecurity, and low self-worth may cause someone to tear another down, but we're hardwired to help one another.

So your options are to give compliments, kindness, help, and feel great or tear someone down and not only look bad but feel bad afterwards. Simple choice. Build each other up.

I'm actually on a mission to gain a few more female friends at the moment. I have a lot of guy friends because they're easier to obtain, but there are so many reasons I'd prefer more girlfriends. Not only will they not try to sleep with me (guys, if you could see the extent of my eye roll right now) or send me unwanted dick picks (put that junk away), but finding a tribe comes with so many benefits.

Women are able to have a different, deeper bond. They'll tell you the hard truth, hold you accountable, and give you an outlet that not everyone can provide. Women respond to stress with a cascade of brain chemicals that causes us to make and maintain friendships with other women. We team up and find strength, comfort, and comradery. I'm totally down for that. Hey, wanna be friends?

LEVEL UP: No One's Thinking

About You

Scenario: Your friends are all out on the dance floor. "Big Pimpin'" by Jay-Z comes on, and your body just wants to DANCE! But you don't. You're too self-conscious to get up in front of all those other people and move awkwardly around the dance floor. Everyone is staring at your every move, and what if you look like Elaine from *Seinfeld*?

I have some news for you. Get off the wall and move those feet because most people aren't actually thinking about you. For real.

Many people are so worried about what others are thinking of them that they miss out on valuable experiences. They hold themselves back, but here's the thing: everyone else is so concerned with their own actions that most people aren't even thinking about one another.

Get up on the dance floor because the folks boogying next to you are thinking about themselves and their *own* Elaine-esk dance moves, not yours! Plus, if someone is watching and judging you, do you think they're going to wake up tomorrow, run into work, and say, "You guys, you won't believe this, I saw someone dancing!" Nope, you'll be a distant memory before they even leave the saloon for the night. So, let's not give up worthy experiences for no good reason.

Here's another example: sometimes my mom doesn't like to come out to dinner with me because I see a lot of my friends, and she believes everyone is thinking, *Look at the mom tagging along with her daughter*, so she misses out on a fun cocktail hour where she'd actually have a great time and meet new people. No, Mom! No one is thinking that. They're thinking, *What an amazing person who is sweet, smart, and engaged. I hope she comes along next time.* Her own worries about other people's possible thoughts (not even real thoughts!) are restricting her life unnecessarily. She's actively choosing to give up on experiences for scenarios she plays out in her mind.

Although my examples are social, this is such a key factor in finding your success. People worry so much about what others may think of their business, product, and plans that they don't follow through. They worry that if they post on social media about their goals, they won't get enough "likes" and they'll be embarrassed. If you're hyper-concerned about your social media likes, ponder this: When this guy named Jesus spoke his truths, some of the people were supporters and believers, but many others straight up mocked him. I don't know much about religion, but I'm guessing if Jesus himself can't get everyone to like him, neither can you. And that's okay. You can't make everyone happy—you're not tequila.

The point is to not allow other people to control your level of success. Your life and the success you aim for is far too important to put in the hands of another person. And on top of that, the fact is that just like on that dance floor, those other people are barely thinking about you or your next move. Please promise me this: If there's something you want to do, do not hold off due to fear of judgment from others. Let go of that power you're allowing others to hold you down with, and you'll see yourself soar to new levels.

"At 18 you worry about what everyone thinks of you.
At 40 you don't care.
At 60 you realize no one was thinking about you anyway!"
—Daniel Amen

LEVEL UP: You're Ready.

F.E.A.R. = False Evidence Appearing Real

Let go of the what ifs. They are not reality. Here's a solid *what if* for you: what if it's not actually a problem and you soar?

A huge reason people stand idle is due to the fear that they're not ready, not educated enough, don't have enough time, or are not an expert. Listen, there are people out there going for it who are a lot less qualified than you and who are *succeeding.* The key is they are taking action. They say an entrepreneur is the one who jumps off the cliff and makes a plan on the way down. It often feels like that. But the point here is to take that first leap. Not everything has to be perfect or in place for you to start building. Things will never be just right, so make a plan, grow some figurative balls, take the leap, and most importantly, remember not to wear your wishbone where your backbone ought to be!

If your fear is failure, that's something you'll simply have to move past it.

Try pinpointing the fear that's holding you back and write it down on paper. Many times, once you see it clearly in front of you, you take away its power and realize this small aspect should not be holding you back. Try thinking about your long-term goals. Is this fear worth giving up where you could be in the next six months?

Practicing different scenarios and conversations that may come up is a great way to take control of the fears and use them to your advantage. Say you want to launch a business, but you're afraid people will ask the hard, uncomfortable questions, and you'll stumble on your answers. Make a list of any and all hard conversations or scenarios that may arise and choose how you'll answer or respond them. Practice those responses and when someone hits you with a hard question, and you'll convey confidence and pride in what you're doing.

Accountability is a great way to push through fears and reach goals. If you simply take the step to tell friends or family what you're doing, you'll then be accountable to make things happen because you know they'll be asking about it at the next holiday dinner.

If you want to achieve big, then you must be willing to risk big. The well-known rental company, Airbnb, launched their business three times. They kept launching and improving (some would call it failing, but they called it an opportunity to improve) until someone finally listened to what they were doing. Simply because your idea or mission doesn't succeed the first few times, that doesn't mean it's a bad idea or that this is the final result. It is the few who use their passion and drive to remain consistent through the failures who will finally reach triumph.

"If you always do what you always did, you will always get what you always got."

—Henry Ford

LEVEL UP: ACTIVATE OPERATION

BRAIN DUMP

When it comes to daily productivity, this is my favorite, most stress-relieving, control-gaining, feel-good activity that I do. It's called a Brain Dump. Okay, stop laughing (you are so immature). But seriously, here's why you need it.

A Brain Dump is when you wake up first thing in the morning, and your to-do list starts invading your head like a swarm of flying monkeys. You end up mentally juggling so many tasks that you forget half of them or are paralyzed from feeling overwhelmed. The key is to keep a notebook nearby. As soon as your to-do storm kicks in, you get those thoughts out of your head and down on paper.

The average person can hold about four things in their mind at one time. Ya'll know you have more than four things to do today! Especially if you're hustling through your days to build a killer life.

Accomplishing a morning Brain Dump allows you to clear these items out of your head so that you're not using up precious neuro resources with that little voice reminding you all day long that your task is undone. It also allows you to organize your must-dos vs. would-like-to-dos, which increases productivity tenfold and eliminates that wasted time trying to figure out what's next. Separating your list into two columns based on importance is crucial for seeing, in a clear way, which items you must fit into your schedule for that day.

A recent study by Wake Forest University found that participants who took a few minutes to actually put a pen to paper with their to-dos had lower stress and anxiety levels *on the spot* and continued to complete said tasks at a higher level (Masicampo and Baumeister, 2011).

Personally, I find it easiest to start by letting my thoughts flow, scribbling down anything and everything going on in my mind. I then break it down into two sections. The items I must get done today, and the items I'd like to get done this week. As you accomplish the must-dos, you can move items over—or if you're list obsessed like me, you can make a new one every damn day. Because I can. Because I'm a list lover and love the feeling of checking something off my list. Boom! Accomplished! Sometimes, I'll even write down something I've already done that day, like "do the dishes," just so I can check that sucker off my list and feel like a productivity badass. Check that! Always remember "done" is better than "perfect" when it comes to your to-do list.

LEVEL UP: Action vs. Excuses

Why do people procrastinate with their goals? Because it's really freakin' easy. We all have at least one area in our lives where we'd like to see change occur. Whether it be our body, career, schedules, organization, patience—the list goes on. But why is it so hard to see these changes through to the end to make them a reality? There is a very simple and straightforward equation to make these changes happen. But change is not for the weak. You must want it and want it badly enough to not give into excuses that derail your goals.

Consistent Action + Time = Change.

It's as simple as that. Small actions that you commit to consistently over time will result in the given change you'd like to see. It's so simple and so boring, but it's the key to your success.

Consistent action may be the MVP here because you need to get up off your butt and do something every single day. But time can't be overlooked. Nothing great will happen overnight or even in a week. We can't disregard the fact that we need to give ourselves time to let these actions build into something real. You may be putting your heart and soul into something every single day and not seeing a visible change, but have faith that if you continue with this over time, you will reach your goal. Remember, success looks easy from the outside.

Excuses

Now that we've figured out the proven process, let's talk about the real obstacle: excuses.

We have excuses for days, months, and even years. Here are some of my favorites when it comes to getting healthy (my weakness). Do any of these sound familiar?

I'll start tomorrow, *for sure*.

I don't have $ for healthy food today.

Everyone's going for dinner, so it's a special occasion. Beer and wings for all!

All the girls are going out; I don't want to miss this action!

I'll do some research and make a plan first (never happens).

I'm too stressed out to even think about that today. F-it, give me a beer and some comfort food.

I just showered and did my hair; I'll workout tomorrow.

The weather is too weathery today. You know what I mean.

It's a cheat day . . . Turned cheat week . . . Turned cheat month.

How about this last one? *I don't have time.*

If you have time to feel bad about yourself, complain, scroll through social media, or watch TV, you have time to build something amazing using that small amount of time each day. I'm raising two children under the ages of five by myself, maintaining my household and the grounds, running my own businesses, and writing a book. You guys, if lil' ole me can do it, you can build something truly incredible if it's important to you. You have the same number of hours in a day as Einstein, Abraham Lincoln, and Maya Angelou. Make your hours and actions count.

If something is truly important to you, you'll make time to fit it in. So next time you find yourself making excuses, try substituting *I don't have time* with *It's just not important enough to me.* See how that makes you feel. Ouch.

No matter what the objective is, our quick brains can come up with a sly excuse on the spot. The problem is, we truly make ourselves believe that these excuses are valid.

One of my favorite slogans of all time is "Just do it." We all know that's the slogan for Nike, but did you know the goddess Nike was a tiny little badass lady made famous for her strength? She had three sisters, Zelus (power), Bic (Force), and Kralas (Strength). Despite their size, sex, and I'm sure one million possible excuses, Zeus called upon these ladies when he prepared to conquer in great battles, and they delivered victory every time. Next time you feel an excuse creeping in, channel the goddess Nike, and JUST DO IT.

Anyways, back to spotting your excuses, calling BS, and making yourself Just Do It so you can witness your end goal in this lifetime.

Try this: Write down your goal. Write down the actions you need to take to reach this goal. If that action doesn't happen, what is the obstacle that stopped you from making it happen? You're not done yet. Next write down the solution to overcoming that obstacle so that the next time you're faced with it, you know your plan of action, and your consistent daily action will not be disturbed.

Here are some points to ask yourself:

—Is this a genuine reason, or is it simply an excuse?

—If this is an excuse, then what is it that I'm currently lacking?

—What do I need specifically that will help me move beyond this excuse?

—What's the next step I need to take right now that will move me closer to my goals?

Beyond the normal day-to-day excuses, there may be reasons why you use an excuse that are ingrained in you from childhood or an emotionally charged event. Recently I listened to Gary John Bishop, author of *Unf*ck Yourself,* speak, and I loved what he had to say about our brains being wired to win. Whether we think we can or we can't, your brain will attempt to subconsciously correct you.

Take relationships for example: Say you had a few relationships that totally bombed, and suddenly, you lose hope and start saying to yourself, "I just suck at relationships, or I get stuck with the wrong people who mess everything up." Once you get this in your head, subconsciously you make small decisions to help you "win" at what you believe. Although you want a solid relationship with a partner, you start being extra aware of problems that aren't really a big deal. Maybe you have a shorter temper, or you make little digs when you should be supportive and understanding. These seemingly small moments of subpar actions carry out the attack and eventual death of your relationship. Congrats, you did it! You proved yourself correct that you won't have a successful relationship. Your subconscious carried you to the glorious state of victory.

This thought stretches across the board. Here's another one I have fallen victim to. My father has a short temper, hot head, low patience, whatever you'd like to call it. After having low patience myself, I decided, well, my father gave me his short temper, and my brain used that as an excuse to subconsciously control my reactions accordingly. My brain set out to make me a winner. But like all things learned, it can similarly be unlearned. I can and have improved my patience, and I'm now able to release that excuse which once supported my unbecoming behavior. Now that I know our subconscious holds these thoughts based on our past experiences, I can use this to see what other areas I'm falling short on in my life and see how I'm "winning" to make them come true.

Adolescents may think, *My parents did a poor job raising me*, so they'll continue to make bad choices to support that. Someone else thinks, *I'm unhealthy and overweight,* so they have that extra cookie, both because they're using it as an excuse to indulge, and your brain makes it feel more doable because it wants to prove you right.

 So where do you feel you're falling short in your life? Is it finances? Health? Career? Relationships? What are you subconsciously telling yourself about these areas of shortcomings? How have your past experiences shaped your thoughts on it? What steps will you take to locate and repair your actions?

Another ingrained excuse is self-sabotage. I dated a guy who blamed every asshole move he made on himself self-sabotaging a good relationship. That was basically a BS excuse for him to do anything he wanted despite how it made me feel. However, since I thought his excuses were a total crock of shitake, I investigated. Raquel Peel, PhD, studies self-sabotage and has a great TedTalk on the subject. What I found from his talk is that it comes down to a basic need to subconsciously protect yourself.

Let's take relationships for example, since that's a common one. You love the person, they're great, but you start doing little things to sabotage the relationship because you've experienced some sort of pain connected with love in the past. Whatever emotionally charged experience we've endured makes our brain say, I've been here before, we got hurt, let's end this now to protect ourselves so we don't end up broken again. And so ensues the small gestures to slowly create cracks in the foundation until the relationship crumbles.

Maybe in an early experience you had a presentation at school or work, and you totally bombed. You were mortified. Now, even though you still work your ass off, you withhold sharing your thoughts in a meeting, procrastinate on big projects, or bomb the next presentation. Aspects of self-sabotage typically feel right in the moment but damage your long-term goal. The thing is, even though we're trying to protect ourselves, we get hurt either way. We do want a successful relationship, career, and life, even though these protective actions tell us otherwise. So, let's choose to be open to the possible pain of the unknown, which is necessary for success in any area, and fire the self-sabotaging body guard we have guarding our actions. If we locate the areas we're struggling in, examine what types of experiences we've had in our past that may be affecting them, then make an active attempt to correct those actions, you can avoid this whole self-fulfilling prophecy game and start to Level Up in these areas.

"He that is good for making excuses is seldom good for anything else."

—Benjamin Franklin

LEVEL UP: THE GAME PLAN

Everything starts with a plan. A plan exposes your goals and dictates the actions needed to get there. So, let's start planning your perfect life.

My favorite way to do this is to take some time to write out my dream life on the left side of a blank page. If my life could look like anything in the next year, or even ten years, what would it look like? This is where you let go of reality and write openly without logistics or judgment. No one must see it, just let your mind flow and the pencil go. If you see yourself in a house in Hawaii, go for it. It's like a vision board with a plan that you can adjust as often as you'd like to keep your actions aligned with your goals.

On the right side, you'll match up the clear actions that will get you closer to this goal. Because as we know, a goal without a plan is just a dream. You'll be amazed at how once you write down a goal and start acting, improvements quickly take form. And when you see these goals coming to fruition, damn, that's exciting.

For example, some of my short-term goals for this year are the following:

Goals	Actions
Happy kids	Actively improve on my patience
Well-rounded children	Take them to see new things locally and sign up for classes they're interested in
Publish book	Write daily, put money aside for publishing
Be healthy, in shape, love my body	Plan out meals ahead, exercise regularly, remember how amazing my body is, no matter the shape
Buy new car	Establish price range, pull the trigger
Have a loving partner and great friends	Keep the positive people who respect and support me, release the rest
Have a happy and positive baseline	Work to train brain to react positively to day-to-day events

But hey, let's open up and go even bigger. What does my dream life look like in ten years?

10 Year Dream Life	Actions
Top selling author, no money restraints	Write every day, add value to people's lives
Own a house on the water	Write daily, make smart financial decisions
Travel more, both with and without the kids	Start a saving account strictly for travel
Host family vacations in which everyone from around the country can come together in one house	Write daily, make smart financial decisions, become an expert on marketing literature, expose myself more—even when it's uncomfortable, keep family and loved ones close and reach out regularly
Find things that make my children's souls sing and help them achieve their passions	Expose them to many different things, listen to what they say and how they feel about each one, if they find a passion, run with it
Be surrounded by great people who make my heart happy	Keep the positive people who respect and support me, release the rest

As you'll notice, even my seemingly farfetched ten-year goals have actions in which I can start taking now to move myself closer to said dream life. Many of them are already in place to achieve my short-term goals.

As stated previously, the simple equation for change is Consistent Action + Time = Change. You can't have one without the other, but if you apply both, change will happen.

Your turn! I know it feels a bit naughty to write in a book but get a little sassy and take a few minutes to dream, write, and make a plan.

Dream Life / Goals   **Actions**

PART 3

RELATIONSHIPS- THE GOOD, THE BAD, THE ONES WHO F-ED UP RELATIONSHIPS:

ON FRIENDS—BUILD A LIFE OF BONUS FRIENDS

Here's the scenario: someone comes into your life—a partner or a friend, and you find yourself quickly depending on them as your primary source of happiness (Which FYI is supposed to be you!).

But *what if* everyone who enters your life is simply a happy bonus at that moment in time? Allow yourself to take all the pressure off wondering if the relationship will work out as your expectations dim. Instead of thinking, *What's that person doing now? Are they the person they say they are?* or *Is this "the one?"* replace it with the confidence of knowing that you make your own personal happiness, and their beautiful presence is simply a wonderful added bonus. What if the end result of any given relationship isn't the end-all-be-all, because the universe, god, source energy, pancakes has a plan and will guide you in the right direction? What if, even though the relationship totally flops in the end, you feel fulfilled because you made the most of cherishing every happy moment that happened, rather than wasting time worrying about what could be? What if you released the fears of the unknown and gave yourself permission to be happy with this bonus friend who is in your life at the moment? Maybe you two revel in this happiness for years to come, or maybe it's just for the moment—and that's ok.

The point is, life is fluid. People come and go. You are in charge of your own happiness. If others come along to brighten your days for a time, allow them to come, and when one of you are ready, allow them to go. Allow yourself to appreciate their gifts to your beautiful life without expectations of the future.

Most religions have takeaways on relationships that can positively improve your life. Personally, I appreciate Buddhist views on attachment. Buddhism encourages independence through non-attachment. Non-attachment is the idea that in order to be fulfilled and happy in life, a person cannot be attached to any one thing because this thing can cause suffering. They encourage one to detach from the idea of a perfect person and holding one's partner to an impossible standard (expectations). If you choose to love this person unconditionally, you love them throughout their changes in life. It could mean they move away, a relationship status changes, their health changes, or income adjustments occur. Side note: this certainly does not mean to withstand any unkindness or abuse, not even for a minute, but more to love a good person fluidly, since life is much like water—consistently and unequivocally in motion.

We set expectations for ourselves and our relationships that lead us to heartbreak. Think of most songs on the radio: they're always strumming on about that one true love or the one who got away. Whether or not you believe there is one true love out there, expecting your next relationship to be some sort of perfect, unflawed, true love is setting yourself up for failure. Take off the rose-colored glasses after watching all those rom-coms you love so much (I know, I love them too). That fairytale mindset can hinder the potential of what the relationship could be. Simply because they weren't the love of your life doesn't mean that the relationship should be trashed in disappointment. You could have just found a great lifelong friend to love unconditionally, which is a pretty amazing thing to have in your life. Give yourself permission to release the *what ifs* and enjoy the person you have in the moment. Life is fluid and always changing, so learn to ride the wave!

RELATIONSHIPS:

ON CRUISING SOLO

Speaking of not depending on others for your inner happiness, let's talk about holding out for a worthy partner.

"I long to find my other half," she says, gazing through the cold glass onto the gray and morbid rain-filled streets.

Girl. Get a hold of yourself. You are one whole-ass woman all by yourself. There's no other half. You are the Whole. Damn. Thing.

If you meet a compatible person who adds some bonus happiness to your life, that's awesome. But never ever should you ever be waiting for another person, thing, or moment to complete you. Mark my words, you're complete without any outside attachments.

If you find yourself spending time worrying about the imaginary "what-ifs" of another person, here's the thing: you have too much time on your hands and you need to take a class, find a hobby, make some new friends, exercise, meditate, or simply better yourself in some way. Your mind power and energy are far too important to be wasted on the what-ifs of another person.

We live in a culture where loneliness provokes fear. You're supposed to be in a relationship, be with family, be with friends, have TV/music on, or basically do anything that will distract you from yourself. The truth is if you give yourself a chance to romance your aloneness, it can be beautiful, calming, and empowering. If we cannot understand and be comfortable with ourselves, how do we expect others to be comfortable with our true selves? Being alone doesn't always mean loneliness. It's a time for us to channel our inner goddess and to understand ourselves in a deeper, profound, and more meaningful way. This is the time when you stop panicking about finding someone else to fall in love with and simply allow yourself to fall in love with yourself. To *learn* about yourself. To *grow* yourself. Fall head over heels *in love with you.*

When you take the time to remove distractions, you'll find some raw emotions that you may have been attempting to cover with the loud noise of busyness. Maybe that's why we're so readily able to distract ourselves all the time; it's easier to distract than to face the raw emotions head on. Sadness is one that most of us have. It's okay to have sadness somewhere deep down there. I'm the queen of *"I'm fine, I got this, I can handle it, I'll figure it out."* But once you remove the distractions, you can truly examine what's happening underneath. For me, it's panic. Panic that I'll be less than what my children deserve. Panic that I won't be able to pay the bills along with any extra curriculars the kids want to do. Hockey gear and dance classes are freakin' expensive, in case you didn't know. It's guilt that I made the decision to get a divorce, which although it was necessary, restricts my kids from seeing their dad every day.

But along with the real, raw, emotions you'll find that you also feel yourself. You'll feel the strength in your soul. You'll see the beauty in your miraculous body and mind. Once you allow yourself to go there, you can tend to whatever unhappiness you may find. Sometimes just realizing it's there and thinking about these hidden scars will allow them to flow away as if you've finally unlocked them to be released from your heart. Afterwards, all of you is finally seen, and you progress with a calm clarity that supports and carries you further in your outside relationships and self-worth.

Love is a remarkable and marvelous thing. But since I'm completely on my own, I'm not about to settle for a mediocre love chemistry, better yet a mediocre partner in life. I can say I'm worth more and saying that is not being self-absorbed or over-confident, it's being healthy. I don't need to settle for something that's less than genuine or a partner that's not my equal.

To me, living the single life is pretty freakin' great. Don't get me wrong, if a guy showed up and turned my life upside down with confidence, respect, and passion, I'd be a happy camper. I love, love. I love hard and I love openly. But until I find the real deal and an equal, I'm absolutely living it up as a single lady, Rockstar-style.

I like the way I live my life. I like having dance parties in the kitchen with my kids while I cook dinner. I like taking a break from the grind and going out for some food and a beer all by myself while I talk to neighboring bar dwellers who always have a story to tell. I like spending my time building my businesses, even if it means waking up before everyone and then working long after everyone is asleep. I love having a huge bed to myself and actually sleeping through the night because there's no snoring partner in it. I like being self-reliant. I'm both the mother and father figure for my children in a typical day, and I run the household accordingly—I'm outside chopping wood and inside cleaning the house in the same day. I enjoy my own company. I make myself laugh all the time; not everyone thinks I'm funny, but all that matters is I crack myself up on the daily, nay, the hourly. In the end, not everyone will gel with how I like to live my life and what my family needs, and that's okay. I'm going to keep dancing my heart out while I cook up some killer tacos, laugh out loud, and love every minute of it.

RELATIONSHIPS: ON LOVE–

THE REAL THING. THE REAL DEAL

HOLYFIELD. THE REAL McCOY.

Whatever you're looking for in a partner, man, woman, pancakes, be sure to hold out for the real deal. It will be worth the wait. Hold out for those whipped-cream topped, homemade maple syrup-covered, chocolate-chip pancakes. I might be projecting, here.

I love Mark Groves's view on love:

> *We're all waiting for someone else to do it first. To choose us, love us, share first, be vulnerable first. We operate from 'I'm closed but you should be open.' See how that's backward? If you always go first, you'll always win. Because your love isn't dependent on others, it's dependent on yourself. It feels scary, right? That's because most of us believe we're lovable if someone else love us, can you love you? Perfect. Can you show up, love all out, and be ready not to be loved back? When we give unconditional love, we invite it in.*

My past has been an I'm-closed-but-you-should-be-open lifestyle, so this totally spoke to me. That's what I was offering, and thus I was attracting like partners in return. I was attracting people who were guarded, scared of real raw love, and unwilling to become vulnerable in order to build something together. I now realize If I want unconditional love, honesty, and vulnerability in a partner, then they deserve to have that from me to begin with.

Listen guys, I'm not holding out for the perfect, mythical, leading role in every romantic comedy. I'm not on the hunt for perfect. I'm not waiting for the one with the chiseled body, perfect smile, big career, love at first sight, spoils me with gifts, life of the party, amazing conversationalist, donates his time to the sick, and sends me around the world on vacations. I'm not saying I would say no to all that, but George Clooney is already taken, so . . . onward and upward.

"What I do require is someone who won't just have another relationship with me, but a partnership
Someone who will listen without judgment and then help me formulate a plan of attack
Someone who values calm, honest, kind communication that allows us to build an unstoppable companionship
Someone with which I can build an empire and then go build a snowman
Someone I know will show up, day in and day out, and will choose me
Someone who will call me on my bullshit but also lift up my farfetched dreams
Someone who will make me laugh because I never want to stop laughing
Someone who can fill me with peace and serenity with a simple touch
Someone who is devoted to our partnership and makes it a priority
Someone who feels like home"
— #PrettyCombat

In a world full of hookups and informal, non-meaningful connections, it's important to stay true to yourself, your standards, your needs, and your self-worth.

We attract what we are, so it's imperative that we build the qualities we're looking for in our partner *first in ourselves*. If you want a loyal partner, you must be a loyal person in your own life with friends, family, and loved ones. If you're aiming for a partner who has qualities of kindness, confidence, honesty, and vulnerability, be sure you're actively walking the walk and not just talking the talk. Just as you deserve an amazing person with these qualities, a good and worthy partner deserves exactly the same from you.

People are hardwired to go after what they want. If someone wants you, wholeheartedly wants you, you will know it. They won't make you feel like an option, make you wonder, or make you chase them. When that person wants you, they'll make you feel like they've just won the lottery, and there's nothing that could keep them away. They will pursue you, love you, and commit to you without hesitation. If this isn't the case, then it's okay. This person will never be a worthy partner for you, so be grateful you acquired this information on where they stand now, instead of wasting time and gaining pain. Give them the old *1, 2, 3, next* and keep building yourself. If someone wants to see you, they'll find a way, find a reason, and make an effort. If it appears they aren't acting in this way, then they may be keeping you as a back-burner option, just in case the main course doesn't work out. And not one person reading this book is a back-burner type of chick. Honestly, you don't even chase your shots, so what makes him think you'll chase after him? Silly boy. #123NEXT

If you have children in your life, it's crucial that you hold out for the great one. This other person stepping into your life will be teaching them, by example, how they should treat their future partner, how they themselves deserves to be treated by others, and how they as parents should treat their children when the time comes. That's a big responsibility for the new partner, and not everyone is capable of properly fulfilling that role.

There's a lot of pressure for mommas out there in the dating world, and it's a hot mess of excitement, weirdness, guilt, and happiness. The pressure is on for a successful hunt that will eventually bring home a kill worthy of your whole family. If I thought dating in college was hard, I've been schooled, because finding a guy worthy of my kids? Few and far between, let me tell you. But for both them and myself, it's so worth the wait because we freaking deserve it. If you suspect a potential suitor is not up to par, give him the #123Next and move on to bigger and better things.

One thing absolutely crucial to a healthy relationship is communication. If I could have God, universe, source energy, or pancakes send you something in this love life, it would be a partner who can openly and calmly listen to your concerns, share theirs, and make a plan to adjust together. Man, doesn't that sound glorious? It seems so straight forward, but it takes a level a of maturity that many seem to be lacking. This is something that can be worked and improved on if both partners are willing to put in the effort. It's important to acknowledge that in order to make a relationship solid, you must both be willing to adjust based on each other's needs. Communication is crucial to locate those needs, convey them, and adjust accordingly. This is an in-depth topic, so we have resources on our site if you're interested in improving yours; however, here's a good way for you and your partner to start improving now during a conflict:

—Avoid using the silent treatment.

—Don't jump to conclusions. Find out all the facts rather than guessing at motives.

—Discuss what actually happened. Don't judge.

—Learn to understand each other, not to defeat each other.

—Talk using the future and present tense, not the past tense.

—Concentrate on the major problem, and don't get distracted by other minor problems.

—Talk about the problems that hurt your or your partner's feelings, then move on to problems about differences in opinions.

—Use 'I feel' statements, not 'You are' statements.

"You deserve someone who is utterly obsessed with you."

—Ella December

RELATIONSHIPS:

ON LOVERS—YOU STUPID, STUPID HEART

The moment you start to wonder if you may deserve better . . . you do.

If it no longer serves you, helps you grow, or makes you happy,

it's time to show gratitude for what once was and have the strength to walk away.

— #PrettyCombat

Darling, today's breakup is far better than tomorrow's divorce. Let's get into the nitty gritty of subpar relationships. Most everyone falls victim to one of these at one point or another. The key is realizing when it's time to get the hell out.

I consider myself to be a pretty intelligent, confident, and strong woman. Basically, I'm awesome. So how is it possible that my heart can be so very stupid? At one point I fell in love with a big, strong man that was amazing, difficult, loving, and full of highs, lows (many), and inconsistencies. I can't even say how many times over our five-month relationship I said, "He's just not good for me. Don't be stupid. It's so clear." And then he would text me, say he loved me, and I'd forget about all that and immediately respond with, *"OMG I LOVE YOU TOO!"* ... W.T.F? You stupid, stupid heart.

What I've learned along the way is that when things don't add up, it's time to subtract.

Juliana Breines, PhD, (2015) proves that love has a response very similar to addiction and should be handled accordingly. Studies have shown that when romantic partners who are intensely in love are exposed to photographs of their beloved, the brain regions that become activated are the same regions that are activated in cocaine addicts when they are craving cocaine.

One strategy in overcoming this addiction to a person is to reframe your thoughts and emotions about that person as if he or she is a cold, clinical biological process, in order to gain a healthy distance.

For example, after a week of radio silence from that not-so-special someone, you feel a wave of longing in your chest and think, *But I really do love him or her . . . I should call right now . . .* Instead, you could simply notice that sensation and think to yourself, *Interesting, there goes my caudate nucleus releasing dopamine and producing a sensation of longing. Okay, back to work.* Easy peasy, right?

During my unhealthy, comfort-food-binge-inducing, five-month relationship, I took the quiz below and failed with flying colors. Flying. Freaking. Colors. You're in an unhealthy/mentally abusive relationship if any of the following apply:

1. You feel the need to change who you are to make your partner happy.

2. You must defend your significant other to family and friends.

3. Nitpicking and criticism — even if said in jest — are constants in the relationship.

4. You're always untrustingly wondering what your partner is up to when you're not around.

5. Your partner makes all of the big relationship decisions.

6. Your sex life is seriously lacking.

7. You want more "me" time—but your partner wants more "we" time.

8. You feel personally responsible for your partner's happiness.

9. Your partner controls who you see and what you do.

10. You find yourself wondering if you're in the wrong relationship.

How did you do? Probably not as poorly as I did, but if your answers resonated with many of those, it's time to put your thinking cap on.

While we're on the topic of tough love, let's chat about some BS nonsense we need to "woman up" and call ourselves out on:

The BS: "They're really trying to be with me."

Girl, if someone wants to be with you, they will find a way to be with you. A person who values you would never put themselves in a position to lose you.

The BS: "It will be different this time."

No, it won't. Don't make me say Albert's overused quote, but okay, if you insist: "insanity is doing the same thing and expecting different results."

The BS: "How can I be sure? Maybe I'm not giving him/her a chance."

You've given them too many chances, and you know it. Know your worth, stand up tall, and be done with the nonsense.

The BS: "Maybe I'm just being overly sensitive because of my last experience."

It's true. If you've been deeply hurt in the past, it can affect your current reactions to situations. But a solid partner will hear what you're saying, acknowledge your fears, and work with you to solve a relationship hurtle *together.*

A relationship takes a lot of give from both parties. You being understandably sensitive to a certain circumstance because you've been screwed over by some unworthy asshole isn't solely your burden to carry in a solid relationship.

The BS: "We talked about it again, and he/she assured me it wouldn't be the same."

Spoiler alert: it will be the same. Insanity is believing that the outcome will be different. Please don't be insane. Be the badass warrior goddess that knows her worth and will not accept any less.

All relationships, even toxic ones, have hidden benefits. Otherwise, why would you stay in them? Identify the perks and determine what, specifically, you are getting from this relationship. Does X make you feel attractive and sexy? Do you like having company? Is the sex great? Once you've pinpointed those needs, you'll know exactly what you need to do to fulfill them on your own.

For example, if you like to snuggle? Rescue a dog. Want great sex? Get a great toy. Need company? Go to a group class or meet up with an old friend. Want to feel sexy? Get your hair done, get a new outfit, and go out on the town. Like the excitement of someone showing interest? Go float around on a dating site. Those Tinder guys will tell you all the nice things you want to hear. Side note: physically meeting them in person, not so recommended. Trust me, I know this from experience.

Here are some points to keep in mind:

—Stop waiting for your partner to change.

—Remind yourself that it isn't your responsibility to rescue your partner.

 —Accept that you are worth more.

—Understand that it will hurt. It will hurt until you recover and realize it was the best move you could have made for yourself.

—Remember that happiness is in your control.

—Know that you're freaking awesome, strong, and deserve the best.

"Sometimes good things fall apart so better things can fall together."

—*Marilyn Monroe*

RELATIONSHIPS: On the Wishy-Washy Ones

Okay, so maybe you're not in an unhealthy, mentally abusive, toxic relationship. Maybe you're just drifting along, wondering if it's worth it to stay with this person.

In every relationship, each partner has needs. When the needs aren't being met, you communicate that to your partner and then work to meet those needs. But sometimes those needs just can't be met. Many times, people stay in a relationship, knowing that their needs aren't being met, because society has us trained that the lesser option is to be alone.

It may be time to move on from a relationship like this if you experience any of the following:

You've clearly communicated your needs, and your partner is not willing to put in the effort to meet them.

You find yourself seeking those needs in others (physical or emotional).

If you have exciting news, the first person you want to tell is not your partner.

You don't feel comfortable asking your partner to fulfill these needs for fear it may make you look needy or emotional. Open communication is everything in a relationship.

The People in Your Life Don't Support Your Relationship—It's easy to say things like, *"My friends never wants my relationship to work out"* or *"My parents don't know what we're like when we're alone."* But the truth is your close friends and family members can see things which someone in love has missed. Their words are certainly not the final say, but don't discard their point of view. Love is blind and ignorance is bliss; the people close to you can see through that for you.

You've Already Put in the Effort to Get This Far, so You Might as Well Keep Trying—You've invested a lot into this relationship. You want to reap the rewards of your investment and not feel like you've wasted your time and effort. But if you've tried to fix the issues to no avail, cutting your losses will save you valuable time in finding what really makes you happy.

You're Trying to Hold on for the Children—Try as you might, your children *will* see and feel your true emotions. If it feels toxic to you, that toxicity will leak and spread into their living area. They won't see a portrayal of true love and support. They will see a broken relationship and a stressed parent. Since this is what they will base their future relationships on, staying together doesn't always mean the healthiest choice for them down the road. Honesty and vulnerability will allow them to have successful relationships of their own when the time comes.

"No relationship is a wasted relationship.
It reveals your needs, so you can grow.
It proves you can love hard, so you know
there are still things out there that set your soul
on fire.
It strengthens your knowledge of self-worth
and exposes the worth of your strength.
It reminds you to let go of the little things
because happiness is an ever-flowing journey.
It gives you the opportunity of a fresh start to
be the best you.
It prepares you to accept that how you love
is not always the way you will be loved.
It teaches you to be strong enough to let go,
and wise enough to wait for what you deserve.
It puts your trust in what's meant to be.
Sometimes not getting what you want turns
into getting exactly what you need."

— #PrettyCombat

RELATIONSHIPS: ON THE D WORD—TRAGEDY TO TRIUMPH

No matter how hard you try to hide the problems in a marriage, once it gets to that point (if you've been divorced, you know that point I'm talking about), it's impossible to portray a healthy relationship, even in front of the people who need to see it most: your children. This isn't your fault. Relationships fade, change, or crumble for so many reasons. If you can't make it work, it's not your fault. From the outside people don't see that you fought like hell to make it work. It simply can't always work. And that's okay. Because on the other side of the darkness that is a divorce, there is a glorious, magical land where all parties can be happy in their new life, children included. If you're able to both put your baggage behind you and make every move going forward with the kids' best interests at heart, there is a strong possibility of reaching that land where you work as a team for the children and leave the past troubles in the past. Did I think that would ever happen when we were in the middle of the worst of it? Nope. But can it happen over time, by putting in the work on both sides? Absolutely. This is something where I would take advantage of the support out there (books, counselors, etc.). We have some resources on our site. In the words of *The Waterboy*, you can do it!

Sometimes you have to walk away, not because you don't love them, but because you love yourself more. I've learned to love the sound of my feet walking away from things that aren't meant for me.

— #PrettyCombat

After a break up, they say the only way to get over a broken heart is to fall in love again. So fall in love with your own damn self! Post break up is honestly one of my favorite times. After I allow myself to understand and accept the situation, I take a minute to be a sad bitch, then get back up and remind myself I'm a bad bitch. This is truly a great time. You build yourself back up, feel powerful AF, and you are free and genuinely happy—a happiness that depends on no external factors. You are solely responsible for your happiness during this time. That, my friends, is priceless. Plus, as a bonus, there's no better revenge than becoming a better, more amazing version of you, that they no longer have access to. Not that we would ever waste our time on revenge.

There's no more freeing moment than when you realize you're not living your life for any other single person but yourself.

RELATIONSHIPS:

ON COCKTAILS—OH ALCOHOL, YOU'RE A FICKLE BITCH AND A HARSH LOVER

For the first part of my life, alcohol was my truest and most trusted companion. We laughed together, we sang together, we danced together through the streets of Boston like the drunken hooligans we were. When I was stressed, it would lighten my load. When I was shy, awkward, and anxious, it would help me fit in. When I had to deal with emotions such as lost loves, heart-breaking family matters, or the guilt of my divorce impacting my children, it helped me push those feelings way down deep and pretend it wasn't happening. It helped me push on through with a smile so I could continue to make everyone else happy. My tried and true companion just "got me." So how could we ever fall out of love?

I've never considered myself an alcoholic, but like my mother gently reminds me, everyone in our family has always "really enjoyed a good cocktail," so be aware and be careful. Different folks define the highly stigmatized word "alcoholic" in different ways. I don't claim to have in-depth knowledge on that subject, but what I do know is that in my past I was never the person to have just one drink and happily head home. Once you get this party train going, it becomes a "freight train of fuck yeah!" and if that train came to a screeching halt, I was usually pissed at the responsible person who ended the fun by going home early. How dare they not want to feel like absolute death at their 9:00 a.m. conference meeting the next day. Bologna.

I'm happy to say I'm crushing in my low alcohol consumption life these days; however, If I'm being straight with you, I'm surprised that I left college alive with the amount of jungle juice and stupid decisions I made. My best friend, roommate, and partner in crime loved to party as much as I did, and I can't even count the number of mornings we woke up and said, "Whoa, is that how we got home? That was dangerous." Or things like, *"Did we ask a random stranger standing outside of the bar to drive us to a McDonalds at two a.m. and then to our apartment?"* But really, did we need to risk our lives with a strange man to score twenty chicken nuggets and all the sweet and sour sauce? I think not. Anyway, I happily leave my mortifying college years in the past where they belong.

But the truth is, you don't have to be going nuts partying every night *or* label yourself an "alcoholic" to realize that booze could be having a negative impact on your life and certainly on your current goals.

After I met my then-future husband in college, he graduated, I left with him, and we stopped drinking for a while. All was well for the eleven years we were together until we came upon our divorce. I was on my own and tasked with the job of meeting new people in a new town. So without a second thought, I headed right down to my comfort place, the local pub, where everyone knows your name. The kids were finishing the school year in Massachusetts while I made us a home in Maine, so I was on my own most every night during this time.

A glass of wine to relieve the stress of the divorce and the move turned into going out a few nights a week to make some new friends in a new town. That progressed into having a cocktail with lunch, thinking, *It's cool, it has OJ in it, so really I'm just being a fabulously fancy lady*. Then eventually onto meeting a guy who loved to drink just as much as I did. We found ourselves looking at the bottle of Allen's Coffee Brandy thinking, *Man, that would be delicious in our coffee. I'll start off the day happy and then really get things done!* It *is* the state drink of Maine, after all. You guys, FYI, you never get anything done after morning drinks. You're welcome for that life-changing piece of hot-off-the-press advice.

That's when I realized I needed to chill the F out. Plus, alcohol has serious calories, and I was becoming less confident by the day. After getting over that alcohol-infused break up (yeah, that mentally abusive one I spoke of before), I cleaned up my act.

I spent most of my drinking years feeling like an inadequate version of the person I knew I should be. I was done with that.

I'm now at the point where I will go out and have a few drinks every now and then to see the regulars who I genuinely love to chat with, but honestly, those empty calories and dollars spent aren't worth it. Often when I have a glass of wine at home, I can honestly say it just makes me tired, sometimes annoyed and catty with people, and I usually don't accomplish my goals for the night. So, consider me and my tried and true companion—fallen out of love, broken up, and better off only seeing each other weekly.

Listen, I'm not trying to rally people to convert them to a cult of non-drinkery. I'm simply saying if it's disrupting your day to day, moving you further away from your goals, encouraging regrettable decisions, wasting your money, making you feel less confident, tired, or unhappy when it's over, then it may be worth it to give the whole week or month off from booze thing a shot. You'll be surprised how often that month turns into a longer period for many people. Oh, and with how many less calories you consume, you'll be looking fine with a capital F.

A lot of people don't entertain this option because they don't want to be a social outcast. Yeah, you may hang with those drunken hooligans a bit less, but you'll attract some new, level-headed, quality people who have the same drive as you. Others don't want to give it a try because they'll feel awkward at events and parties. Yes, you'll be forced to learn how to feel comfortable in your own skin. That sucks at first. But you do learn, and once you do, you start to feel like an unstoppable badass. You'll also learn how to make yourself genuinely happy without depending on booze. Your answer to a stressful situation will go from *Omg, I need a drink!* to learning how to control your stress and emotions, finding a solution, and handling it like a boss.

You also don't have to be a self-proclaimed alcoholic to use some of the support that's out there to drink less or stop drinking. You don't need the alcoholic label to take a break from it. I'm certainly not an expert on addiction, but we do have some resources on our site.

RELATIONSHIPS:

ON THE TABOOS OF THE

ALMIGHTY DOLLAR

This relationship is sometimes considered taboo to discuss openly. The truth is, it's not greedy to want to be in a stable relationship with money. It's something you're trained not to talk about openly with others; however, it's simply smart to want to be financially educated and prepared for what life will throw at you—whether it be buying a house, kids, or an unhealthy shoe obsession. It's even okay to put yourself in a position where you can do things like enjoy life and take a damn vacation now and then.

Think about this: how many times will you meet up with your girlfriend for lunch and chat about an exciting upcoming date or new pair of shoes? Okay, now how many of those lunch dates are spent discussing investments, financial strategies, and getting smart about the almighty dollar? Probably slim to none. We are smart women, so it's interesting to me that many of us are lackadaisical when it comes to getting serious and even aggressive with our finances. We might let the partner take control or just settle for a paycheck-to-paycheck lifestyle. Stocks, bonds, savings, and investments are a foreign language to many of us. I cruised down to Boston to meet up with Lauren Higgins, a well-known financial planning expert, to give us the low down on falling in love and building a comfortable, stable, and exciting relationship with *money.*

Lauren agreed that women have an interesting relationship with finances:

> There's actually this thing called the Money Taboo, and it it's all about the discomfort women feel when talking about money. Women will talk about anything with their friends, but they won't talk about money. For many women, talking about finances feels intrusive, embarrassing, or inappropriate. But the thing is, most of us have the same questions and concerns. Many women define financial security as being able to provide for their kids, themselves and their family. It's not a number in an account at age sixty-five. It's being able to juggle all we are asked to juggle while walking the tight rope. I encourage women to ask questions, talk openly about concerns, and get familiar with your family financial picture so you can be an active participant in the plan.

Okay, so we're getting over ourselves and getting uncomfortable as we dive into the unknown in order to become dollar savvy. First off, like everything else, we need goals and a game plan to get a feel of the big picture and exactly where we want to end up.

Lauren explains what that means.

> *Financial planning is about you. It's about fusing your goals and wishes with financial-planning best practices. In order to create your own plan, start by writing down your short-term goals. What do you want to achieve in the next six to twelve months? Do you need a new car? Do you want to go on a vacation? Are you trying to pay down a student loan? Whatever it is, write it down and assign a dollar amount to the goal. Then, identify goals for the next twelve to twenty-four months. Do you want to buy a home? Do you want to start your own business? Do you plan on starting a family? Again, write it down and ballpark a cost for that goal. On the starting a family bit, of course it is not a one-time expense, but consider what expenses you will pay in that first year or two. Will you still work? Will your partner work? Will your maternity or paternity coverage be paid or unpaid? What will daycare cost if you do plan on returning to work? These are just a few of*

the financial considerations that should be a part of your initial planning.

After thinking through your short and intermediate goals, think about those longer-term goals five- to ten-plus years out. When do you want to retire? Do you plan on paying for a dependent's education? Do you want to purchase a second home or pay off a mortgage? Once you have a sense of your goals, their timeframe, and the potential cost, you can create a realistic plan that sets you up for success.

Depending on your goals, their timeframe, and their cost, you will want to match the investment vehicles you use with that goal. For example, your emergency account of three to six months' worth of expenses should be in cash. Boring, stable, ready-to-access cash. However, for money you aren't planning on using for five-plus years, you should probably move that out of cash and into something with more growth potential. Before jumping into any investment, spend some time understanding what it is, how much it goes up, and equally important, how much it can go down.

You guys know I love a good chart. Let's do it:

Within the next year:

GOAL	AMOUNT NEEDED TO ACCOMPLISH

Next twelve–twenty-four months:

GOAL	AMOUNT NEEDED TO ACCOMPLISH

Next five–ten years:

GOAL	AMOUNT NEEDED TO ACCOMPLISH

It's critical to think of your future self as a priority in your currents self's financial picture. A few ways to ensure that happens is to automate your savings and schedule it to deposit early in the month. Look for ways to direct savings through payroll contributions, linked checking accounts, and other mechanisms to remove the monthly execution from your (likely) lengthy to-do list. Failing to make it a regular occurrence may compromise your ability to follow through.

Start early. Today. Wealth is built over time and with discipline. The time element is key, and there is a way to leverage time to your financial benefit. Starting to save early allows your savings to compound, and the impact can be staggering. Take for example a twenty-year-old who saves $1,000 per year for twenty years and earns 6 percent per year. At age forty, the individual stops contributing to this account. At age sixty-five, they would have an account balance of $X. Take another individual who starts saving at age forty. In order to have an account balance equivalent to that of the first individual, they will need to save twice as much for twice as long. Make your money work for you and start saving today. Concerned the amount you can save may be too small? Ask a local financial planner to run the numbers for you, and you will be amazed at what a regular deposit can grow to.

Okay, Lauren, I hear you. The time is now. But I'm a visual learner so let's take a look at the importance of starting to save now vs. when we have the extra funds when talking average savings rates:

Scenario A: Starting Early
- Save $1,000 per year for 46 years
- Total Contributions = $46,000
- Portfolio Value at 65: $226,508

Scenario B: Playing Catch-Up
- Save $3,825 per year for 26 years
- Total Contributions = $99,450
- Portfolio Value at 65: $226,273

Save $1,000 / year starting at age 20				
Age	Beginning Balance	Additions (End)	Interest Rate	Ending Balance
20	$ -	$ 1,000	6%	$ 1,000
25	$ 5,637	$ 1,000	6%	$ 6,975
30	$ 13,181	$ 1,000	6%	$ 14,972
35	$ 23,276	$ 1,000	6%	$ 25,673
40	$ 36,786	$ 1,000	6%	$ 39,993
45	$ 54,865	$ 1,000	6%	$ 59,156
50	$ 79,058	$ 1,000	6%	$ 84,802
55	$ 111,435	$ 1,000	6%	$ 119,121
60	$ 154,762	$ 1,000	6%	$ 165,048
65	$ 212,744	$ 1,000	6%	$ 226,508
Total Contributions	$ 46,000			

Save $3,825 / year starting at age 40				
Age	Beginning Balance	Additions (End)	Interest Rate	Ending B
20	$ -	$ -	6%	$
25	$ -	$ -	6%	$
30	$ -	$ -	6%	$
35	$ -	$ -	6%	$
40	$ -	$ 3,825	6%	$
45	$ 21,562	$ 3,825	6%	$
50	$ 50,417	$ 3,825	6%	$
55	$ 89,031	$ 3,825	6%	$
60	$ 140,705	$ 3,825	6%	$ 1
65	$ 209,857	$ 3,825	6%	$ 2
Total Contributions	$ 99,450			

FIGURE 1: THE PERSON IN SCENARIO B HAS TO SAVE OVER 2X AS PERSON IN SCENARIO A TO CATCH UP. WHILE MOST PEOPLE WOULD ARGUE IT IS EASIER TO SAVE AT AGE FORTY WHEN THEIR INCOME HAS GONE UP—RELATIVE TO WHEN THEY WERE TWENTY—OFTEN THERE ARE COMPETING GOALS INCLUDING MORTGAGE, KIDS, INSURANCE, ETC. SO THE COMPETITION FOR EACH OF YOUR DOLLARS IS A LOT HIGHER THE LONGER YOU WAIT TO SAVE. WORK SMARTER NOT HARDER!

Cool, I like money, so let's start investing now. Exactly how much should we be saving each month? Let's talk budgeting with Lauren.

In order to take control of your day-to-day spending, you first need to understand what it looks like. Creating a budget can be an incredibly helpful exercise because it allows you to analyze current spending, create targets, and hold yourself accountable. The hard part is figuring out where to start. It can be helpful to start by looking at the last six to twelve months of spending. Credit and debit cards typically provide a year-end summary to account holders. Start by taking those year-end statements and grouping your expenses into a few primary categories. For example: housing, debt payments, food, utilities, clothing & shopping. As you get more comfortable with budgeting, you may want additional categories, but starting simple can keep the exercise from consuming all your free time!

Once you know what you have been spending, you can determine if your current spending allows you to save toward the goals you've outlined for yourself, such as planning for retirement, college, vacations, or home improvements.

If your current spending patterns do not allow for what you need, review those discretionary categories to determine how you can move in a direction that will enable you to save toward your goals. This may not happen overnight, but having a defined plan will make it far more likely to happen.

Why, hello chart.

Use these items below as reference or cross them out and add your own. Let's see how we're doing financially. This may hurt for a minute, but it's an imperative step in the process of realizing where we are now, and the steps we need to take in order to set ourselves up for a killer end game.

Basic Monthly Budget:

Item	Monthly Cost
Rent/Mortgage	
Electric	
Heat (gas/oil)	
Transportation/gas	
Debt (Car Payment, Credit Cards, loans)	

Cable, phone, internet

Groceries

Discretionary (hair, clothes,
nails, dinner out)

TOTAL MONTHLY
COSTS:

TOTAL MONTHLY
INCOME:

I will adjust monthly spending by changing
_____ in
my monthly budget.

I will add $_____ to my savings each month.

Okay, I have my extra dollars set aside. What exactly do
I do with them? Before you choose your investment

account, Lauren says it's important to keep these things in mind:

> *Don't leave money on the table! Many employers offer a match on money contributed to a company retirement plan. The catch? The match is only offered if the employee puts money in too. It is worth reviewing your employee handbook or plan-summary document to determine if you might be leaving free money on the table. If your company does offer a match, this should be the first place you focus your savings efforts.*

> *Have money in your own name. For a multitude of reasons, having a bank account or credit card in your own name can be invaluable. For some individuals, this can give them peace of mind that in an emergency they can provide for themselves. In the case of a separation or divorce, this could be the difference of having access to money for legal counsel or bills while marital assets are frozen. For others, it's simply being able to buy a gift (or splurge!) without scrutiny. Whatever the reason, whatever the relationship status, having access to funds in your own name is empowering and responsible planning.*

Diversify. The age-old saying of "don't put your eggs in one basket" is particularly true in financial planning. One of the more common financial missteps is to invest heavily in one or two companies, which exposes your savings to unnecessary risk. In the absence of knowing which company, sector, or even country will do well and which one will not, seek diversified investments that are low cost and clear in their objectives. If you aren't sure how to select investments, this may be one area a financial planner can be helpful. An annual review of your investments is prudent to make sure your investments aren't too risky relative to your goals and time horizon.

Since the finance world is always changing, it's hard to choose the best options for your money. A financial advisor is usually the best bet for a game plan, and many of them will meet with you for a no-cost consultation before you make any commitments.

There are many options for online investing that allow you to get started with a low minimum investment.

These numbers will not be accurate as time goes on, but here's a snapshot of what we're looking at today as far as a few Robo-advisor options:

Wealthfront—Their fees are reasonable at 0.25%, and you will need $500 to get started, so keep that in mind.

M1 Finance—If you don't have that $500 starting balance, M1 Finance has a minimum starting balance of $100. They charge no commissions or management fees, and the user-interface is very user friendly.

Betterment—If you're starting out with less than $100, you may want to consider Betterment, which has no minimum starting balance whatsoever. Like M1, it's also great for beginners as it provides a super simple platform and a hassle-free approach to investing.

Mutual Funds—A mutual fund is a type of professionally managed investment that pools your money with other investors. There are investment securities that allow you to invest in a portfolio of stocks and bonds with a single transaction, making them perfect for new investors. Many mutual-fund companies require initial minimum investments of between $500 and $5,000.

Roth IRA—An individual retirement account allowing a person to set aside after-tax income up to a specified amount each year. Both earnings on the account and withdrawals after age 59½ are tax free.

Cookie Jar—You heard me. If these vehicles for investment are making you nervous, stick to a good old cookie jar kept safely in your house and slip a few dollars into each day or week. They key is to start saving. Today.

There are many other avenues for investing. Even a simple savings account at your local bank will be making money for you with a typical rate of about 2.25% (again this number is always fluctuating). The best thing you can do is set up a free appointment to chat with a professional financial adviser to get a full view of your current options. Go get 'em tiger!

RELATIONSHIPS:

ON CHILDREN–

MRS. HULK-POPPINS

"I'm not a regular mom. I'm a cool mom."

—*Mean Girls*

Yeah, I'm just not a cool mom. If I had to describe my parenting style it'd be more like a hard-ass Hulk mom with a dash of Mary Poppins. It takes a sane person to live seamlessly between two personalities. While scrolling through Facebook, I saw a post from my favorite hilarious mom blogger, Amy Weatherly. It was just so damn spot on in portraying a normal day in our household, and it went a little like this:

> *Me first thing in the morning: Good morning, baby. How did you sleep? Did you have the sweetest dreams? Gosh, I love you so much.*
>
> *Me ten minutes later: HURRY UP. I DON'T KNOW WHERE YOUR SHOES ARE. THEY ARE NOT MY RESPONSIBILITY, BUT YOU'D*

*BETTER FIND THEM
AND YOU'D BETTER FIND THEM FAST, OR
ELSE. I SWEAR . . . NO. NO, YOU MAY NOT
HAVE COOKIES FOR BREAKFAST. YOU
GET WHAT YOU GET. I AM A PERSON,
NOT A BREAKFAST BUFFET.
IT IS TIME FOR SCHOOL, THOUGH. STOP
MOVING IN SLOTH MODE AND
GOOOOOOO!*

*Me at drop off: Bye, honey. Have a great day at
school. I can't wait to pick you up.*

*Me ten minutes later: HURRY AND GET OUT
OF THE CAR. PEOPLE BEHIND US ARE
WAITING.*

*Me at pickup: Hi, sweetie! How was your day? I
want to hear all about it! I missed you!*

*Me ten minutes later: NO. WE CANNOT
STOP AT MCDONALD'S FOR A HAPPY
MEAL. STOP CRYING. YOU JUST HAD ONE
YESTERDAY. SOME KIDS GO THEIR
WHOLE LIVES WITHOUT EVER GETTING
A HAPPY MEAL. I WILL HAPPY MEAL YOU
IF YOU DON'T STOP FIGHTING. BE
GRATEFUL FOR WHAT YOU HAVE. DO I
NEED TO STOP THE CAR, BECAUSE YOU
KNOW I WILL. STOP WHINING NOW.*

Me at bedtime: Goodnight, baby. I love you so much, and I had the best day with you. I am so so so proud of who you are and who you are going to be. Sweet dreams. Jesus loves you.

Me ten minutes later: GET BACK IN BED. YOU DON'T NEED ANOTHER GLASS OF WATER AND THE BLANKET YOU HAVE IS JUST FINE. IT'S NOT SCRATCHY. JESUS BETTER LOVE YOU, CAUSE YOU WILL BE IN BIG TROUBLE IF YOU GET OUT OF THAT BED ONE MORE TIME.

Me ten seconds later: Okay, I love you. Goodnight. BUT SERIOUSLY—DO NOT GET OUT OF BED AGAIN. I love you so much. BUT SERIOUSLY.

Yup. Spot. Freaking. On. Can anyone else relate to the dual personality insanity we call parenting? It takes equal portions of being the strong arm and giving great hugs. But honestly, I'm more than okay with not being the "cool mom." I'm not in this to make friends or to try to look good. I'm in this to raise two humans that will better this world, not be complete assholes, and live a happy, fulfilled life. *That* takes both a little Hulk and a little Poppin's action—a little lose your shit and a little extra snuggle time.

I'm not saying I have this parenting thing down. No one does or ever will. No one will ever perfect themselves to a point where they can then perfect another person. The world is always changing, which means the environment we try to control and perfect is always changing along with it. This is a good time to grab hold of that guilt we spoke of before—about not being the perfect parent (or perfect anything)—and rev up that engine, get cruising at ninety mph, throw that guilt out the window into an empty field, then go ahead and set that field on fire. It's a complete waste of energy to suffer through trying to control something that will never be complacent and is incapable of being perfected. Aka, parenthood.

What I do know, though, is children love and crave rules, boundaries, and schedules. They do. I've gotten the occasional compliment on my children's behavior, and that's *not* because I have it all down, not by a long shot. Like, not even the longest shot ever. It's straight up because I'm an asshole of a parent sometimes. Sorry, not sorry.

I have a stare so fiery and fierce it could make a full-grown man drop his bag of potato chips and start cleaning up his toy trucks. I march into the day mentally armed and prepared to shut down any disrespect, tempers, or whiney behavior. I'm not here to be their friend; they'll have plenty of those if they're raised to be kind, respectful, and confident. I'm here to educate their little minds, show them how to love hard, and how to think for themselves. I'm here to ensure they're capable of being self-reliant, compassionate, and hold a high value of self-worth. To guide them through their feelings, which they'll convert into thoughts and needs, and then how to properly convey those needs through calm, clear communication in order to obtain what they desire (aka no tantrums). To help them accept a circumstance that they don't necessarily like with poise and gratitude. To cultivate happiness that comes from inside themselves rather than external factors. To be polite, courteous, and good-natured. To know the importance of punctuality, responsibilities, and dependability. Because if I weren't here tomorrow, they must be armed with the tools necessary for success to not only survive but *thrive* on their own.

This can't be done in the form of buddy, friend, amigo. It can't be done by being *only* the nice mom or *only* the hard mom. It takes a controlled dual personality lifestyle. So my kids don't like me sometimes? Don't care. In the end they're going to thank me for being overly strict at the appropriate times. You're welcome in advance, MacKenzie and Cal—from your sometimes annoyingly proper but always loving mother.

I also must be a little more Hulk than some other moms because I'm the mom and the dad in our normal day to day. Growing up in my household, my father was the enforcer (remember that hot temper?), and my mother was the sweet nurturer (don't let that fool you; she's tough as nails). I play both roles, and I'm okay with that, because it's necessary.

I find it interesting to hear a lot of talk going around about the youth today and how their subpar behavior is outrageous. People complain how the youth have changed; they're disrespectful, lazy, and entitled. I agree that a lot of people out there really suck. But aside from special circumstances, guess who taught many of these ungrateful adolescents a lot of their current suckery? Truth bomb: it's the parents. I may lose some friends here, but the reality is that many of these kids weren't born assholes or born kind and courteous. They're not born with a laziness gene or born knowing how to work hard to get what they need; but the great thing here is if you have a child who is exhibiting "unsavory" behavior, it's not too late to adjust. It's never too late to guide them to a shift in mindset that will set them up for a greater and much easier life.

It will be harder for sure, but worth every painstaking mile of reworking how this great child thinks and acts. As we know from the mindset talk, everything that is learned (behaviors) can be adjusted. Our minds are not sedentary; they are always growing and improving with work. The catch is, kids cannot think at the maturity level needed to break a behavior cycle, let alone decide to do anything about it. This means it's 100 percent up to the parent to put in the work, but hey, we're up for the challenge!

So what does "putting in the work" look like?

1.   Draw a line in the sand.

Boundaries seem pretty basic, right? I suppose the key here is to realize that boundaries are not an option to enforce when deemed necessary. If you have a set rule in your household, it is the rule consistently, day in and day out. Giving in to these boundaries will put the control in the hands of the child, which cracks the foundation of respect in conforming to the rules. Young children do not have the capability to make all the correct decisions for themselves, and that's why we're here.

For us, one consistent boundary topic occurs at dinner time. We have a hard rule of "you get what you get, and you don't get upset." Because guess what? They're lucky to get just one thoughtfully made meal with our crazy schedule, never mind multiple menu options catering to each family member's specific taste pallet. But I've noticed that if I listen to my kind heart and give in just once, they'll be in a full-blown sprint to gobble up that inch and take the whole damn mile—all while sporting a smug smile and a golden medal at the finish line. The next night at dinner, they won't eat because they think they'll "win" and I'll give in again. Boundaries, which may feel disruptive at first, create a level of respect and control that kids want and need. In this chaotic world, boundaries are calming to children.

2. Routinely keep routines.

Routines fall under the same category of aiding in comfort and introducing a sense of control for a child. When they know what to expect in their day, it helps them to be calmer and more grounded. Routines also cultivate responsibility. If each morning they know the routine is to wake up, eat breakfast, bring their dishes to the counter, and brush their teeth, they feel accomplished, proud, and self-sufficient. Not to mention, man, will your mornings be more relaxed.

3. Goodnight, sleep tight, don't let the temper tantrum strike (this is my new favorite nursery rhyme, BTW).

With all that children have to learn and grow from each and every day, it's no surprise that their little brain needs some serious rest. They're learning social skills, empathy, and etiquette. Their bodies are constantly moving, exploring, and reaching. Their minds are processing emotions and how to properly react. Sleep is crucial for healthy brain development, never mind to avoid the overtired tears that ensue when the child inevitably drops his piece of popcorn on the floor, and the world as we know it comes to an end. Just like with staying strong on your rules and boundaries, the firmer you are with a set bedtime, the easier they abide as time goes on. If your child seems easily frustrated, quick to tear up, or even angry, more sleep is a sure-fire way to ease their discomfort.

4. Time to party! I mean, *play.*

"Children don't say, 'I had a hard day . . . Can we talk?' They say, 'Will you play with me?'"

—Lawrence Cohen

This quote is just so damn true. We're so busy with our tasks, works, chores, social media scrolling, that we assign the duty of playing to our children, not realizing that we need to allot some playing time of our own to get down on their level and communicate in a way more readily accessible to them. Getting down on the floor and playing with your kids may be a stressor to you because your brain is firing off a hundred adult tasks you should be getting done in that time, but it's important to realize that they *need* us to get on their level with them to hear what they're experiencing in their day, locate their needs, and work with them accordingly.

5. Get *out* of my house!

Meryl Davids, author of *Enlightened Parenting,* sums this up perfectly:

> Movement through active free play, especially outside, improves everything from creativity to academic success to emotional stability. Kids who don't get to do this can have so many issues, from problems with emotional regulation—for example, they cry at the drop of a hat—to trouble holding a pencil, to touching other kids using too much force.

Insert: mic drop.

6. Get to work.

It certainly doesn't make things easier when you ask a young child to do a chore. Even if they're pumped to be doing it, it takes longer, and you typically have to covertly tuck and roll into the room to redo the chore after they've finished. But there's plenty of research to back up why it's important to suffer through watching these little humans do these tasks incorrectly. Things like higher self-esteem, responsibility, better ability to deal with frustration and delay gratification, and higher success rates at school have all been related to integrating chores early on in life.

Research by Marty Rossman (2002) indicates that "the best predictor of young adults' success in their mid-twenties was that they participated in household tasks and responsibilities when they were three or four." Talk about setting them up for success!

7. Switch it up.

Have a dance party, do yoga together, go for a walk, have a scavenger hunt, learn a new skill together, or have a picnic in your yard. Make an active attempt to change up your normal get-everything-done mentality, and instead choose to engage in experiences that will create a deeper connection between you and your kiddos, as well as create memories that they can hold onto forever. Children value nothing more than quality time with their parents. If you feel like you're tearing them down by enforcing new rules and hard boundaries (you're not, but you may feel that way), you'll build them right back up with quality time. All they want is you. Pure, undistracted, full-on eye contact, intently listening, YOU. Kids will never remember their best day of television, but they will forever remember the real connections and out-of-the-ordinary, even if simple, experiences they shared with you.

No one is a perfect parent. No one will ever be a perfect parent. All we can do is try to set our children up for success—even if it means slowly losing our mind in the midst of those special little moments of love.

"If you have never been hated by your child, you've never been a parent."

—Betty Davis

RELATIONSHIPS:

ON CHILDREN—

AN OPEN LETTER TO THE MOTHER, SUPERHERO, SAVAGE, MULTI-TASKING GENIUS, EXHAUSTED KEEPER OF EVERYTHING

You amaze me. Mothers work the equivalent of two and a half full-time jobs—ninety-eight hours per week. No freaking wonder it's exhausting. Now, the guys out there are probably saying, "That's just a crock of rigged data. I help out a whole darn lot."

Good job, buddy. But for some reason most of the daily responsibilities fall on the mom. The invisible workload of motherhood is overwhelming and doesn't get acknowledged often enough.

Invisible labor is the sum of all of the micro decisions and choices mothers make on a moment-to-moment basis that have become expected over the years by their children and perhaps even their partners.

Doctor appointments, open houses/teacher conferences, playdates, magical holiday festivities, prescriptions for the entire family, permission slips, emotional support, baby books and memories, enrolling in extracurricular activities and getting them there, keeping the peace between siblings, birthday parties including when, where, and what to buy, birthdays and important dates of all extended family members including the husband's, purging the constantly outgrown clothes, donating and replacing them with new better fitting attire, playing Santa for the whole family, man, I could literally write another entire page of additions to this list of Mom Duties, but I bet you get the point.

You are the person. The one who knows how to stop tears in their tracks, depending on which child is in need, the one who knows how to make them feel safe and confident in any situation, and the one who knows their favorite, well, everything, and you didn't become this person because you were born with a special set of skills. You became this person because you put in the hard work, blood, sweat, tears, and many trial and error failures to learn what each person needs. You put in the work. And YOU deserve a gold freakin' medal and a year of back massages because you take all of this on your shoulders without being asked to do so—and possibly without a partner who works equally as hard to learn how to become "the person" to relieve a portion of your duties. You're amazing.

Without thought, you place everyone's needs before your own, because you are Mom. You're required to handle it all while saying, "I guess I can go one more day without a shower." You feel like you're trying to keep your head above water and possibly like you're failing to succeed. In reality, you are the only one who calls struggling to handle all of this "weakness"— anyone looking in from the outside would call this strength. The strength of a savage momma bear going all out to protect, guide, and persist until her family can thrive, all at the price of her own self neglect. I salute you. ♡ -Ali

While we're on the topic, let's check some hard, proven facts that came up in a study about momhood. They found developmental science is replete with studies on the impact of mothers on their children, but little is known about what might best help caregivers to function well themselves, so they decided to change that. Their study found the following:

> —Nine in ten women said they felt solely responsible for organizing schedules of the family.

—Seven in ten women said they were also responsible for other areas of family routines such as maintaining standards for routines and assigning household chores.

—Most of the women also felt it was chiefly them who was responsible for monitoring their children's well-being and emotional states.

—Eight in ten said they were the one who knew the children's school teachers, and two-thirds indicated they were the person who was attentive to the children's emotional needs.

—The invisible labor of ensuring the well-being of children showed "strong, unique links" with women's distress and mental illness.

—The study's findings suggest women who feel overly responsible for household management and parenting are less satisfied with both their lives and partnerships (Suniya S. Luthar and Lucia Ciciolla, 2015).

"My children cause me the most exquisite suffering of which I have any experience. It is the suffering of ambivalence: the murderous alternation between bitter resentment and raw-edged nerves, and blissful gratification and tenderness."

—Adrienne Rich (1995, 21-22)

PART 4–EXPECT THE UNEXPECTED

Written by Nicole Parmiter

EXPECT THE UNEXPECTED: WELL, THAT WASN'T THE PLAN

Life is never what you expect—well, isn't that that whole damn truth. No matter how amazing something looks from the outside, the behind the scenes are filled with trials, tribulations, and confusion.

Back in my glory days, I had the honor to be part of one of the greatest organizations in professional sports. I'd stand on the sidelines every Sunday in my white high-heel boots, cheering on one of the best teams in the NFL. Sun shining on my face, Tom Brady in my direct view, and dawning the coveted Pats cheer gear while professional photographers snapped shots of me. It sounds magical doesn't it? You're right, it was an experience I still hold close to my heart.

But behind the scenes was so very different.

Professional cheerleaders are expected to have a certain level of perfection. A certain look. There were weekly weigh-ins where we all stripped down to our bra and underwear, only to stand there secretly looking each other up and down, wishing we had that girl's boobs or another girl's butt. Countless hours of trying to perfect yourself in every way possible while everyone around you judged you. I can't count the number of rumors I heard that I had gotten a boob job. Newsflash: my boobs were all mine. Well, all mine with a whole lot of padding up in there.

Through all the judging and rumors, I was forced to learn how to focus on the positives. That doesn't come easily in your early twenties—let alone at any time in life. It's something you need to teach yourself, practicing it until it becomes second nature. It's mindset. It takes a lot of heart and control because it's much easier to settle into the negatives of any given situation. To get down on yourself for the way you look, or for what someone said about you. To beat down on yourself for not being someone else's version of perfect.

Fortunately, this opportunity brought many positives, from working with wonderful charities, visiting hospitals, trips overseas boosting moral and supporting our troops, to lifelong friendships with some strong, smart, and beautiful women now-turned badass bossbabes to partying with A-list celebrities.

By focusing on the positives, you eventually drown out those negatives, and they become memories you can laugh at and find some sort of twisted joy in. Plus my alleged fake boobs really looked great back in the day, so I say let the haters hate and embrace yourself!

"Often those that criticize others reveal what he himself lacks."

—*Shannon L. Adler*

It's so true that when someone else is criticizing you, typically behind your back, that it usually comes from a place of his or her own insecurity.

What it all boils down to is how comfortable are you in your own skin? How happy are you with your life? If you focus on bettering yourself, knowing your weaknesses and owning your flaws, there won't be a reason to criticize others. You'll be able to embrace the success and beauty in others and know that we all have different things to offer. This is a seemingly simple task, but unfortunately, it's something our society struggles with. When it seems like someone has it all together, and you feel the jealousy moving in, remember that each person has their own inner struggles unknown to the outside.

I challenge you to become self-aware. Really learn who you are, what your strengths are, and where you lack. Are you the person who glances behind you to be sure you're holding the door for the next person, or do you walk right through without a care in the world about who is behind you? Be that first person. Hold those doors, make eye contact with the person at the checkout counter, return your shopping cart, and say hi to a stranger.

Instead of dwelling on the messy hair of that disheveled and exhausted mom at drop off, tell her she's doing a great job with all those young kids, and that you love her kicks. The ripple effect that occurs from small acts such as those are exactly how we can make a positive change, not only in others but most importantly within ourselves. Your energy will shift and take shape in a beautiful way—in turn, you'll begin to love and appreciate yourself and others in a whole new way.

"Be the change that you wish to see in the world."

—Mahatma Gandi

EXPECT THE UNEXPECTED:

FROM BALL-PLAYER BUMS TO

WIPING BABY BUMS

After retiring at the old age of twenty-six, I went from
high-heel boots, staring at football players' butts, to high
heels in the corporate world, kissing executives' butts.
Talk about life not being what you expected, right?
We've all got to make a living, though, so I muscled on.
Throughout my career, I finally found a company who
cared for its employees and made me feel like part of a
family. I managed an apartment community (talk about
having to kiss a lot of ass—you learn the real type of
crazy that people are when you work where they live). I
built a team of five people and we became family.

I enjoyed that freedom and independence of not
needing to rely on anyone else, in a financial sense—and
man did I love my high heels. When deciding to go back
to work after my last maternity leave, it was a struggle,
but I knew I had to do what I felt would make me the
best mom possible. So, I traded in my days with my
boys for my days with my guys—you know, that family
I mentioned before. My work family.

Until one day, we weren't family. A fight between employees became a betrayal that turned into me losing my job. The manner in which I lost my job was dramatic and heart wrenching, and to top it off, I wasn't emotionally or mentally prepared for what was to come.

Four kids under four at home and zero support system around. How in the world was I to find the positive in this? I had been in the corporate world for twenty years, essentially, and now I was getting the violent shove into stay-at-home mom status. I traded in my high heels for flip flops and yoga pants. Wiping butts full time rather than kissing butts. Who knew that as a parent you spend so much damn time wiping people's butts? Kids should come with a warning label about that.

Momming is hard. So damn hard. And when you add severe depression and anxiety, it can sometimes feel like you're living in a nightmare. Losing a job that was so much more than a job altered me in a way I can't describe.

I found myself in situations where I would lock myself in my room and contemplate whether or not I deserved to live. Contemplate if my children would be better off without a mom who loses her mind for no reason at all. The pressures of doing everything not to royally screw up four other humans was building, and I just wasn't sure I could take it . The simplest daily tasks weighed heavier than I ever could have imagined. As I had learned earlier in life, I knew I needed to keep telling myself to focus on the positives—not just for my kids, but for me.

To top off my parenting journey with whipped cream and a sour cherry on top, I felt more judged than ever. As if raising tiny, helpless beings isn't stressful enough, you get to listen to your cousin Becky's sister's best friend's aunt by marriage question every move you make AND throw her two cents in on how you should be parenting. Here are a few comments I actually received from real humans—most of whom were strangers.

"How are you going to do this? It's your first child and you have no clue what you're doing." I'm pretty sure no one knows what they're doing when it comes to bringing home a tiny human for the first time. Hell, I had four and I still had no clue what was going on half the time in those first few months. But you live and you learn, just like anything in life.

"I hope you decided to do the right thing and breastfeed your child." Actually, nope. I formula fed. All four of them. And I realize they all should have grown a third arm or turned into part unicorn or something, but actually, they are handsome, healthy, incredibly smart children who adore their mama. But thanks. If I ever have a fifth, maybe I'll "do the right thing."

"You have three kids under three and you're pregnant again? Didn't anyone teach you about the reproductive system?" Why, yes strange gentleman I am ever so kindly making small talk with at the gas station. I am well aware of how babies are made, and maybe, just maybe, I'd like even more than four. Maybe, just maybe, my reproductive system and life choices have nothing to do with you at all. Yeah. Maybe that.

FYI, don't post a picture of your child in a car seat unless you want half-a-dozen "expert" opinions on what you're doing wrong. Don't complain about your child's fifteenth tantrum of the day, or else you'll have to read "enjoy these moments" literally an uncountable amount of times. And don't you dare ever ask for advice on, well anything, because it will end up in some weird debate between Betty and Sue about whether or not pull-ups should be used for potty training and why it did or didn't work for them. For the love of god, I beg of you, don't ask for advice. And when you do, don't say I didn't warn you!

So just how do you focus on the positives? How do you not let that negative energy in?

I say let it in, at least to some extent. Use it as a driving force to prove people wrong and to show yourself just how great you are. Because you are, in fact, great. Screw that, you are better than great; you are amazing.

In this era of social-media fakeness we all live in, that isn't an easy task. You get a highlight reel of the "perfect" moments, and in turn, you compare yourself to others without even realizing it. I choose to keep it real on the internet. To share my ups, downs, and in-betweens. Now, I'm not saying to air all your dirty laundry, because let's be real, some of that shit should be saved for a better platform like *The Jerry Springer Show*. But by sharing not only some of the crazy-ass things that happen in a house of all boys, but also my inner struggles—and boy do I have plenty—I received an outpouring feedback. I received private messages from a few people who struggled, and in one case, some pretty solid postpartum depression. People thanked me for putting myself out there because it was helped them to know that they were not alone.

You see, we've lost so much genuine relationship building due to this new world of social media. We've lost a sense of reality and true community. We find ourselves trying to create the perfectly themed birthday party and stressing to the max, when let's be real . . . No. One. Gives. A. Damn.

So my advice to you is keep it real. Stop trying to be the picture-perfect human and free yourself from the pressure of social media. Once you train yourself to release the idea of perfection, that heavy weight will lift off your shoulders. Share the ridiculous mess of toilet paper or wipes that your kids tossed all over the room, or the destroyed pillows that your dog chewed to the point where you weren't sure if it was a pillow or an animal. Toss the filters that give you flawless skin and own your laugh lines (Let's agree not to call them wrinkles, k?). Free yourself.

"If you're always trying to be normal, you will never know how amazing you can be."

—Maya Angelou

I may have gone from Super Bowls, fancy parties, celebrities, and high heels to messy buns, tantrums, wiping butts, and cleaning up vomit. So much vomit. And while at no point was any of it what I ever expected it to be, I wouldn't trade what I have for the world.

I've learned to refocus that negative energy, soak up all the positives, and start living a life where I feel free. You know, until my tiny tribe members order twelve snacks a minute, demand their milk cups, and start throwing tantrums like they're going out of style because the wrong TV show is on. Then I may have a moment or two, but hey, we can't be perfect, right?

I release the negatives and refocus on my happiness. I pause, take a few deep breaths, force myself to find at least one positive in the situation (Even if it's something ridiculous like, "only three of the four kids vomited! Win!"), remind myself of something I'm grateful for, get some endorphins flowing with exercise (even if it is doing a few pushups with four kids climbing on my back), or blast a song I'm diggin' these days. We are in control of our minds, and even though this is not what we planned for, we can make it fabulous by taking control, releasing the unplanned negatives, shifting the energy, and dictating our mindsets. You are in control of this crazy, unplanned, amazing life.

PART 5

IT DOESN'T HAVE TO BE LIKE THIS

Written by Jennifer W. Boucher

IT DOESN'T HAVE TO BE LIKE THIS:

I SEE YOU

I see you. Yes you, the one in the terrible marriage. The one suffering from postpartum depression. The one who would rather stay home and drink in private than have to cut back in front of judging eyes. I see you, the one dating the wrong men on purpose to ensure nobody gets too close to you. So there is a reason for your demons. So it is always them and never you. I see you in the dead-end job. I see how frustrated and unappreciated you are. I see you, the bored stay-at-home mom. Wondering if this is it? and then immediately shaming yourself for feeling that way.

I'm wondering when you're going to change. When you will decide you've finally had enough of hiding from yourself. Giving the world one version while being disappointed with the other version: your real self. Your real self is a beautiful soul who deserves to be shared with the world. Yet sometime in your life, someone told you to adjust her a bit, to fit a mold. And the more adjusting and nipping and tucking you've done, the more you've lost her. And yet the older you get, the more she is screaming to be let out, to be re-introduced to the world. And yet you continue to silence her because you've learned that there are things we are supposed to do, and there are ways we are supposed to do them. Alternative methods get frowned upon, questioned, rejected, at times. I am here to tell you that this is no way to live, and it doesn't have to be this way.

I was so fortunate to learn this early in life . . . you know, that it doesn't have to be this way. In fact, I was able to find a workaround to pretty much every situation I wasn't a fan of. My first memory of this was when I was four years old. I went to a Baptist nursery school in a well-to-do suburb of Boston, where every child was expected to participate in the reenactment of the Nativity scene. Most little girls were thrilled to dress as angels or sheep (don't get me started on that metaphor) and prance around the stage. But I was not most little girls. I was small, scrappy, and convinced I should have been a boy. Much to my parents' chagrin, I demanded the shortest haircut possible and my brother's hand me downs. They settled on the ever popular—and practical according to my dad—bowl cut and made valiant efforts to find me rugby shirts for girls (thanks Benetton!) in order to keep the questions to a minimum.

So naturally, when the parts for the nursery school Nativity scene were being given out, I wanted to be Joseph. When the tall, austere Miss Deborah told me I couldn't be Joseph, I very quietly asked why not.

"Well, because Joseph is a male character so he will be played by a boy. Diedrich is going to be Joseph. Would you . . . like to be Mary?"

With her pursed mouth and narrowed eyes, you could tell she didn't want me to be Mary, but she had to offer. Nope. I wanted to be Joseph. For days the negotiations ensued. You could be a sheep, a camel, a beautiful angel! Not interested. My parents were brought in for meetings, but they had lived with me for a full four years at that point and were already exhausted. Finally, I offered a compromise. I would be Joseph's brother. Clearly this was not an ideal solution, since, well, Joseph didn't have a brother. But I wasn't budging. When show time came, everyone was slightly confused as to why there appeared to be four wise men onstage, but I was thrilled with my performance—and that I was able to rewrite history.

Now imagine that you were able to be as bold as a four-year-old, refusing to be coerced into playing a part you couldn't relate to. You have not yet been exposed to other people's opinions, major consequences, and harsh judgment. All you know is what you want and don't want, and you're not afraid to ask for it.

What would you do then? Would you leave that marriage? Quit that job? Go back to work before your maternity leave was over? Because the power that propels you to make those decisions was instilled in you as a child but was slowly stripped away over time. You owe it to yourself to take that back. Remember where you came from and what you thought you deserved before other people started interfering.

IT DOESN'T HAVE TO BE LIKE THIS:

A BUCKET OF DREAMS

No more than a year or so later, my family was taking a trip to our favorite spot, Captiva Island, Florida. They owned a timeshare there where we would meet new friends and then reunite with them year after year. It was my happy place, and I was determined to have my best summer ever at age six. However, my dad had other plans for me. He was a seasoned traveler, a multi-million miler with Delta and would often fly first while my mother, brother, and I sat in coach. That would be economy if we have any millennials reading this. And back then there was no economy plus. Just straight economy. But they still gave out peanuts! Anyway, my dad is a guy who loves rules, abhors clutter, and may suffer from a touch of OCD. Therefore, we were only permitted to bring one suitcase and one carry-on bag aboard. Before that was even a thing.

Now this was a real problem for me as a hoarder of all things. Especially tiny things. I was trying to figure out how on earth I was going to cram my new treasure chest and all of its accouterments into a carry-on bag with all of my other stuffed animals and books that were necessary travel companions. You see this treasure chest was actually a sand pail that came with a ton of shovels, pots of gold, and bricks for sand castle making. It would undoubtedly score me no less than seven new friends on the beach this time around. But as we were packing, my dad would stomp through the bedrooms barking, ONE carry-on bag! JUST the essentials!

If I didn't know any better, I would think he had a secret gig with the TSA based on his travel schedule and how passionately he felt about this rule that he imposed upon us.

I laid all of my treasures out on my bedroom floor and studied my bounty. I was already accounting for the haul of seashells, sea glass, lucky sea beans, rabbit feet, and other necessary nonsense I would acquire while there. I realized I needed to be clever about this. And fast. Like most sand pails, my treasure chest came with a removable handle that allowed me to loop nearly all of the tools through it, freeing up most of the space inside. Once that train started moving, I thought about what else could be looped. Zippy the monkey, grab on with your Velcro hands! Look at all of my friendship bracelets—clearly my new friends will need to know about those. Onto the handle you go. You should have seen the look on my dad's face when I came bounding down the stairs rattling like poor Sandy, the dog from Annie, with a string of cans tied to his tail. He was both furious and in awe as I stood there smiling proudly. My mom touched his arm, "Bill, you did say one, and well technically, it IS one carry on. . . . "

It took Adult Me a long time to learn what Kid Me knew so well. It was a time in my life when I kept telling myself to put on my game face. I could "do this." But what was I really doing? I was lying to myself. I was depriving myself the happiness I deserved by pretending to be content with what society told me I needed. Doubting myself, second guessing myself. Yes, I did that for years. What was wrong with me, why couldn't I just be happy with this incredible life, "on paper?" Maybe nothing, I finally learned. Maybe I just don't belong "on paper." The irony, coming from a writer.

When I finally knew it was time to make a move and make a HUGE life decision, I braced myself for a tidal wave. I knew it would be big and scary and awful and painful. I knew I would doubt and second guess myself more than ever, but how would I know what was right and true if I didn't move? That wave hit me, crashed over me, tumbled me to the bottom, rolled me around, shot water up my nose, sand up my butt, had me gasping and grasping, uncertain as to which way was up and which way to move. But when I finally saw the light, I kept reaching for it until I broke the surface. And only then did I get my first glimpse of serenity. It hurt to move, but I did it. And I resurfaced.

And you know what deciding to make that move, that huge life decision, taught me? That there is a workaround for everything. Things can be hard without being ugly. I've learned that there is no playbook for your unique life. There is no script for a person who has never walked this earth before. Yes, that is you I'm talking about.

Why was it so easy for me as a child to reject no as an answer? To understand that there are far more than two ways to do something? I have had to channel that scrappy little gal a lot lately, and she has been serving me well. The simplest thing I can think of is that I was always one to question things. Why can't I be Joseph? Why can't I bring all of my humanly possessions on an airplane? Typical little kid stuff that my kids now torture me with. The mistake the adults in my life made was leaving out the specifics, which left room for my imagination. Okay, so I can't be Joseph, but I can certainly be his brother! You know what they say, worry is a misuse of imagination. I rarely worry because I am so busy imagining. And what I imagine are ideal scenarios. Constantly. What do I really want? What would make me so happy? Well why can't I have that?

So back to you. You will try to tell me that you're not exactly certain as to what is wrong. That may be true—or you may be in denial. So the first step is to identify the issue: boredom, unhappiness, stagnancy, frustration. What is causing it? How long can you remember being afflicted by it? Does this involve other people? Children, a husband, a boss, a family member? Even if the answer is yes, you must always start with you. Do a deep dive into when you were your happiest, most free, most creative, most amused and tickled by life. Sure, it may not have been a time where you had tiny people whining and hanging on to you 24/7, or before you hitched your wagon to a grouchy spouse or took a job with a condescending boss. It may have been entirely circumstantial, but how did you feel then and why did you feel that way? Because guess what? You can recreate that.

But first you must ask yourself: Am I willing to change? Am I willing to do something big and scary? Am I ready to not just step but leap out of my comfort zone? The same comfort zone that is boring, unhappy, stagnant, and/or frustrating? Yet safe and comfortable.

I say leap because sometimes that is all some people can do. You know the type. If they can't sprint it, they won't run it. But for other people, these are small steps that can be taken one week or even one month at a time. Think about what kind of "Band-Aid person" you are. Do you rip it off in one fell swoop or do you inch it off painstakingly slow? While I don't believe in wasting one precious minute in this singular life we've been given, I do believe in being patient, deliberate, and certain of what it is we're feeling and seeking. Spend a month identifying your issue. Wake up every morning and start journaling how you feel at several intervals throughout the day. At the end of thirty days, you will see a clear pattern as to what it is you're feeling and potentially why you're feeling that way. It may sound mundane and tedious, but it is truly groundbreaking information that you will begin to uncover.

It could be hidden at first. You could very well be blaming a bad job on an unhappy marriage or vice versa. You could think being a stay-at-home mom is painfully dull, yet you haven't gone out and immersed yourself in mommy and me classes or new mom socials. Don't get me wrong, those aren't exactly the things that dreams are made of, but they do put a particularly nice shine on mommy-hood. At least in the beginning.

You must start talking to people. Start sharing what you're going through with someone you connect with. Now this may not be your best friend or your mom or your sister. In fact I can almost guarantee it won't be. This may be that girl you see on social media, posting the vague memes that speak directly to your soul. Or the quiet woman who catches your eye at the gym for how desperately she seems to be working her body to escape from something unseen. Or the mom at pick up, gazing out her window, dreaming of a life she may never dare to step into. Whenever someone on social media dropped a truth meme (seemingly) directly into my feed more than twice, I would reach out to them. Nine times of out ten it was a match—we were going through the exact same thing, and, fortunately for me, they were going through it six to twelve months before me and became my "catastrophic life event" mentor.

So what is that thing for you? That thing that you wish you could change or overcome? That thing that is pulling at your heart. That thing that keeps you up at night and wakes you early in the morning. That thing that sometimes takes your breath away in its enormity that you just can't seem to face. Because you talk yourself out of it. You watch other people and compare yourself to them. You listen too closely to society and how things "should" be, that you tend to forget that things should be and feel right . . . to you, not to anyone else.

Everyone is suddenly riding the Maria Kondo wave of only keeping items which spark joy, but they are forgetting to do this in their real life. They are complacent, willing to be mediocre, and their dreams are just that: dreams, in their head, in their darkness, just out of their grasp because they are not willing to reach a little farther. What if we held onto the intangible items that sparked joy as tightly as the concrete items?

I was considering this connection between the concrete and intangible items after I had the sweetest conversation with my ninety-one-year-old Aunt Therese the other day. She called to thank me for the birthday gift I sent her—rose petal bath salts and a pair of fancy pajamas—and how they were so luxurious that she was going to save them to enjoy on my birthday the following month. Now, Aunt Therese is one of the sharpest ladies I know, and as someone who has taught me so much in my lifetime, I decided it was time to share some of my own wisdom with her. I asked her to use them right away. She deserves to feel fancy all the time, and I don't believe in saving things. Not to be morbid, but when we really have no idea how much time we have left, we really need to be having the bath and wearing the pjs. She agreed that she would, then quoted scripture as she always does, and finally put out a wish to the universe that more people would continue to be so open with one another. To be receptive to others' spirituality, to be brave enough to say what you're feeling, and then to relish what comes your way just by opening yourself up to others.

I see this a lot actually. We feel each other out. We wait to see how people will be receptive to us before we open up. And that is normal and natural, of course, except for the fact that we are often incorrect in our prejudice. When I was going through my catastrophic life event, I shut people out who may have helped me in ways I couldn't imagine—because I couldn't imagine how someone could help me if they didn't understand what I was feeling. But do we necessarily need to mimic someone's pain in order to understand them or be there for them? The answer is a resounding no. When you hear anecdotes or read stories of people who comforted others during hard times, it is often those who did or said something very simple. It wasn't always the people who had been there, although as I said earlier, those are some life warriors right there so hang on to them. I know I tend to react to people the same way I like to be handled, and that is often a mistake. I appreciate a wide berth, lots of quiet time, limited phone calls. If my friend is hurting, they may require something entirely different. I need to be receptive to their needs and not just what makes me comfortable. We will only know what this method is by asking and by acting on it. By trying different things. By making that move.

IT DOESN'T HAVE TO
BE LIKE THIS:
BEFRIENDING YOUR DEMONS

Something that I was fortunate enough to learn in early adulthood came about in a very shocking and unexpected way. I spent a wonderful afternoon with one of my coworkers, strolling through the streets of New York City, having clam chowder at Grand Central Oyster Bar, and chatting it up with her through the secret passageways in the walls of Grand Central Station. A quintessential day in the city, I had an exciting new date to look forward to that night, and my heart was brimming. We returned back to our offices at Memorial Sloan-Kettering Cancer Center to finish our day, and at five o'clock on the dot I left for an eyebrow waxing appointment a couple blocks away.

I was crossing 41st Street with the light and noticed a large bus making a turn toward me. I picked up my pace a notch and reached the other side. I had barely ascended the sidewalk when I heard a noise that I will never forget, yet could never describe. I turned in time to see a woman pinned beneath the rear wheels of the bus. Instinctively I ran and crouched down below the bus to be with her, to hold her hand. She was in and out of consciousness, but mostly out. Someone was already calling 911, the driver was hyperventilating against the side of the bus once he realized what had happened, and all I could do was be with this stranger in what might have been her final moments. The ambulance arrived in minutes and she was taken away to a fate I never learned. I stood on the sidewalk, staring at the street where everything changed in a matter of seconds, and all I could see was her crumpled cup of coffee, splashed all over the road.

Shell shocked, I continued on to my appointment and then home, where life went on. I showered and dressed and headed out on the town for the evening. I tried to block the event out of my head, but I would see things and hear things that would send me into fits of crying out of nowhere. Movies with death scenes were no longer tolerable. Loud noises or spilled drinks would shake me up for days on end. I lived this way for months, wondering what was wrong with me.

Finally someone suggested I speak to the head of our HR department, a sweet older woman called Trudy who had the warm, wise look of an owl. I sat down in her office and cried softly as I recounted the events of that day.

She gazed at me so lovingly through her round spectacles and said, "Tell me, have you ever experienced something similar to this?"

Bewildered, I said, "Well, no not really except . . . I did see my brother get hit by a car when I was six years old."

"Were you alone that day?"

"I wasn't," I responded, "but my mom did have to leave me to ride in the ambulance to the hospital with my brother."

She explained to me that this was a trigger event, and it was bringing back those old feelings of trauma and being alone. Feelings that I had never worked through before. Once I understood that, I was able to move forward in addressing those feelings, and suddenly the world wasn't so scary anymore. Do you believe that fighting your demons can be as simple as understanding where they come from? Because now I do.

Too often we suppress things with the hope that we can outrun our feelings or experiences, when in reality, if we do face that scared, alone little girl, we can make progress and get on with our lives. Things aren't so scary anymore, once we decide to stand up and fight those feelings, rather than run from them. And it wasn't until even later in life that I was able to fully appreciate this healing process that I unknowingly stumbled upon:

1. Admit there is a problem.

2. Share what you're going through with a trusted source.

3. Allow help from a trained source.

4. Uncover, face, and work through those demons with support.

IT DOESN'T HAVE
TO BE LIKE THIS:
I SEE YOU, BRAVE WARRIOR

A year and a half ago, one of my college roommates that I had lost touch with reached out to me. She was quietly following me on Facebook and finally felt compelled to let me know that my posts were resonating with her. But it didn't end there. She went on to say how her life had taken a dark turn, one she never saw coming, and of course one that those who loved her and knew her never saw coming either. She was struggling for years and nobody knew because of the shame she was unable to let go of.

She sent me this message:

"I just have to say how proud I am of the journey you have taken. I am not going to say you're the best mother, wife, friend, professional, etc. Those are titles we give to ourselves and put enormous pressure on ourselves to be the best at them, and at times it can destroy us in doing so. I love seeing you take time to be mindful and realize that enjoying today while you are present is much better than remembering it tomorrow.

I love how honest you are about the fact that getting a "Never Late to School" certificate may not be as important as your sanity. And I love how when you get to a point of "this is enough," you know to stop and breathe and reset. I don't believe that anything would have changed the course that my life took, and I believe that I am where I am supposed to be for a reason. But I think if I had seen some of your posts during my darker days—again not that it would have changed my course—it would have given me some relief from some of my guilt and shame. I am proud of you, and I think you are helping lots of your fellow friends out there just by living a good, healthy, balanced, and mindful life. Well done my dear friend, love you always!"

I read her message with tears streaming down my face. I never knew she even noticed my social media updates, much less that they could have meant anything to her. I had no idea that being a little goofy, a little self-deprecating, and 100 percent real about what goes on in my life might actually take the pressure off someone else trying to fit that Pinterest-mom mold. People do notice you. They hear you and they see you. What you put out there may mean the world to someone, even if they never tell you. I was so grateful that she took this opportunity to tell me, and I couldn't reply fast enough. We exchanged messages for several months, and I truly felt as though I could save her. As a serial networker, I made a mental tally of all the people near and far that would be a resource to her, in one way or another. I vowed to drive hours to meet her for coffee and continue the dialogue. All I needed to do, I thought, was continue the dialogue. That exchange was so pretty on paper, but it just wasn't enough.

A few months after we had lost touch again, I was stunned to see her obituary posted on Facebook. The photo was haunting. It was her high school graduation photo, a time when life should have been so light and hopeful. Before all of the heaviness that she shared with me. Yet her eyes looked dark and almost tearful. She wasn't smiling. Only in death could I finally see her silent scream for help.

She tried her best to live her life on paper, yet she didn't belong there. None of us do. We can be so pretty on paper, but then we can be crumpled so easily. Tossed away.

So let me rephrase how I started. I see you. I see how brave you are, beneath your fear. I see you with the tiny flashes of light and wonder in your eyes that can be stamped out and reignited in the same breath. I see you just below the surface—timid, shimmering, and beautiful. I can see the dreams running through your mind clear as day. What if it didn't have to be this way? you keep wondering. And it doesn't. Because I've lived it and I came out on the other side.

A special person once told me something that resonated deeply with me.

Your life on the other side is so beautiful that you can't even imagine it yet, because you are still so stuck. It is like you are holding a compass, upside down and in the wrong hand. You need to flip that compass over and transfer it to your other hand. Because I promise you, you are going to get there, to the other side, and when you do it is going to blow your mind and you are going to wonder what took you so long.

PART 6

WHAT'S NEXT

WHAT'S NEXT: Your Turn to Grab A Pen

You are armed with the tools to kick ass and create the life you really want. You've always been equipped with these tools, but now it's time to act. I've included some practices to guide you toward jumpstarting the life you crave and deserve! Take some time to think about each question and write out your answers. Let's get clear about what you want!

List three things you're grateful for:

_____

_____

_____

List three things that excite and set your soul on fire
(passions, hobbies, people, activities, topics, etc.):

_____

_____

_____

List three things you want to change in your life (career,
friends, health, finance, mindset, family time, etc.)?

_____

_____

_____

Write out a paragraph about your dream life. Let
yourself be unrealistic and truly DREAM. If you had all
the money in the world, what would your perfect life
look like?

_____

_____

_____

_____

_____

_____

_____

GAME PLAN: Now that we've gotten clear on some things we need and need to change, let's find the steps to take action and get closer to making a life you love your reality.

Goal   **Actions**

What is your first goal that you will take action with?

_____

_____

List Five affirmations:

Phrase these as if they have already happened and include clear goals.

Examples:

I am strong, confident, and smart.

I'm a great mother, friend, and partner.

Money flows to me freely and abundantly.

I'm grateful for my _____ (even if you haven't obtained it yet!).

I'm proud of my success on _____.

_____

_____

_____

_____

_____

List Five activities you'll complete DAILY and what
time of day you plan to conquer them:

Example: drink X glasses of water, affirmations, focused
child attention, exercise, work on passion project,
meditate, etc.

_____
_____

_____

_____

_____

Notes:

_____

_____

_____

_____

WHAT'S NEXT:

TOUGH LOVE SIGN OFF

They quickly learned not to take her kindness for weakness

Or her silence for ignorance.

For if you throw her to the wolves, she'll return leading the pack.

— #PrettyCombat

We have reached the end of the book and the beginning of your opportunity to take the bull by the horns (figuratively; please don't grab a bull's horns; it rarely ends well) and dominate your life.

Tell me, are you going to grab the wheel and be in control of your life or let the seas crash around you and simply be victim of the storm?

Ingrained deep in our soul is the desire for growth, exploration, and forward motion. But this is not where we feel safe and comfortable. Controlling life with tactical domination will never feel comfortable. The first important step toward success will not feel comfortable. Steady comfort is where the unsuccessful couch dwellers hide, and as Bob Dylan would say, that ain't me, Babe! He might've used that in a completely different context, but po-tae-toe, po-tah-toe, right?

So let's make a goal to step up, woman/man up, and feel completely and utterly *uncomfortable.* Requesting that big promotion will be uncomfortable. Sharing your new business idea with the world will be uncomfortable. Learning to improve at your weaknesses will be uncomfortable. But discomfort is where the big wins happen. Discomfort is where people begin, grow, and succeed. Your parents used to be the ones who made you do the uncomfortable things like clean your room, write thank you notes, do your homework, and have proper conversations, but if you're reading this book, it's not your parents' job anymore. The only person pushing you to do these life-improving, yet uncomfortable actions is you. You're never going to feel like getting up early to accomplish, passing on pizza for rabbit food, having a hard conversation about deserving a raise, or completely turning your life upside down with a new business or career, but if you want to be the one steering your life in the direction you desire, then you need to be the one to challenge yourself to be uncomfortable. What's the first thing you choose to be uncomfortable about to build the life you love? Do it today.

Go out there and be the poised, savage, peaceful, scrappy, educated, dreamer that you know you are deep in your heart. Be unwilling to settle for the mundane and mediocre. Find what it is that sets your soul on fire and harness your passion to persevere, conquer, and obtain. And do it all with a big smile because you've freakin' got this.

Xoxo

—Ali, Pretty Combat

The End.

A big shout out and thank you to my people!

I owe so much of what I have to the support of my two little ones, Mackenzie and Callan. They push me to be a better person each day. Every business I've started, they're there, hands on, being a part of it all. The photo for the cover of this book was taken by MacKenzie (6) and lighting by Cal (3). I hope that having them be hands on in all of these "family" businesses will show them that you can start with nothing and build something beautiful with a little hard work and passion. I appreciate them for forcing me to put my money where my mouth is and live as an example, by actively striving to be a kind, respectful, and genuine person. I appreciate that every single day they give me an opportunity to practice on improving my patience. Most of all, I couldn't live without the pure joy and kindness radiating out from their smiles each morning. MacKenzie and Cal, thank you for holding me accountable and making me the person I am today!

Thank you to the three people in my life who always blindly support my business decisions (whether they think they're a good idea or not). My mom, my dad, and my best friend, Dolly. No matter what my next venture is, I know you'll be there in the front row cheering me on, and your support means the world to me!

A giant thanks to the people who added so much value to this book. Guest writers Jennifer Boucher and Nicole Parmiter, Financial expert Lauren Higgins, Editor Tiffany White, funny and impactful stories from Katie Wood and Amy Weatherly, and help with the book writing/publishing process from Erin Neuhardt LeBlanc. Ya'll rock my world.

Meet the guest writers!

I'm honored to have the incredible Jennifer Boucher and Nicole Parmiter each write a guest chapter in Pretty Combat. These are women I greatly admire, and I feel they add real value and perspective with their words. All three of us work in business consulting, life-improvement training, and are moms to some crazy, happy, amazing, little humans. From sitting on boards of organizations to pro-football cheering, these are two brilliant and passionate women who I'm beyond honored to share my pages with.

I met these impressive women in a professional capacity, as we're all entrepreneurs, but quickly took note of our similar stances when it came to sharing our sometimes inappropriate, raw, real-life posts on social media. We are not Pinterest moms, we may not have the perfect lifelong marriage, consistently pristine children, or fit into the cookie-cutter image of how we should live our lives—professionally or otherwise. But we're scrappy as hell. And the truth is, life isn't always pretty. Often, it's a whole lot of down and dirty combat while simultaneously shining our pretty smiles and happy souls to the world. Because whether we always believe it or not, we got this.

What we do know for sure is that we have a common goal with our posts: to connect, uplift, and support. Using social media is our little way of taking action for good by offering words that could possibly reach someone who could relate and hopefully take off the pressures of life, no matter what their situation may be.

The three of us set out on this mission, not to swim in a pool of coins like Scrooge McDuck (not that it wouldn't be awesome) or even to achieve great fame, move to Hollywood, and marry Mark Walberg (also awesome), but to offer up a part of ourselves to affect, help, or add value to this community—to move this world in a positive direction and give strength. All three of us can certainly agree we could have used some outside strength at one time or another along this crazy journey. That's why we put a whole lot of time (and of ourselves) into this book. If you find any takeaways, quotes, ideas, or facts worth sharing, please share the love with your own network. It may find its way to someone who needs it at just the right time!

 Jennifer W. Boucher is a freelance writer who has been mistaken for a New York Times food critic on more than one occasion (and snubbed by Modern Love on more than one occasion). She is an Rfx Circle & Lexus Achiever with Rodan + Fields and was named the 2017 "Woman to Watch" by the YWCA Bergen County. Jennifer's first job at Memorial Sloan-Kettering Cancer Center ignited her passion for philanthropy, which propelled her to seek creative ways to give back with the New York Junior League and Foundling Friends. She now holds a board position with the Social Service Association of Ridgewood and Vicinity and is an advocate for Hayden's Heart and Stop CMV. Jennifer loves to cook and considers herself her own personal sommelier. She currently lives in New Jersey with her three children and their Boston bulldog, where she embraces the beautiful mess of it all.

 Nicole Parmiter is a wife and Mom to four devilishly, handsome boys, Gavin, Dylan, Bryce & Tyler; living in the suburbs outside of Hartford, CT. Nicole is a former professional cheerleader for the New England Patriots. During her time with the organization she participated in countless charitable events, performed overseas for the troops with Blues Traveler and attended back to back Super Bowls in which the Patriots won. She is an avid football & sports fan, lover of music, one of Tom Petty's biggest fans and an entrepreneur. She's currently devoting all she has as a stay at home mom to her boys.

Please check out our site for resources and information!

www.PrettyCombatBook.com